D1707932

Valode & Pistre Architects

Layout and cover design  SANDRINE RONDARD - PARIS
Lithography  PHILEAS NUMÉRIQUE - PARIS
Printing  FGB - FREIBURGER GRAPHISCHE BETRIEBE, FREIBURG I. BR.

A CIP catalogue record for this book is available from
the Library of Congress, Washington D.C., USA

Bibliographic information published by Die Deutsche Bibliothek
Die Deutsche Bibliothek lists this publication in the Deutsche
Nationalbibliografie; detailed bibliographic data is available in the
Internet at <http://dnb.ddb.de>.

© 2006 Birkhäuser - Publishers for Architecture,
P.O.Box 133, CH-4010 Basel, Switzerland
Part of Springer Science+Business Media
Printed on acid-free paper produced from chlorine-free pulp. TCF ∞
Printed in Germany
ISBN-13: 978-3-7643-7200-2
ISBN-10: 3-7643-7200-1

9 8 7 6 5 4 3 2 1

www.birkhauser.ch

# Valode & Pistre Architects

PHILIP JODIDIO

BIRKHÄUSER — Publishers for Architecture
BASEL • BERLIN • BOSTON

# Contents

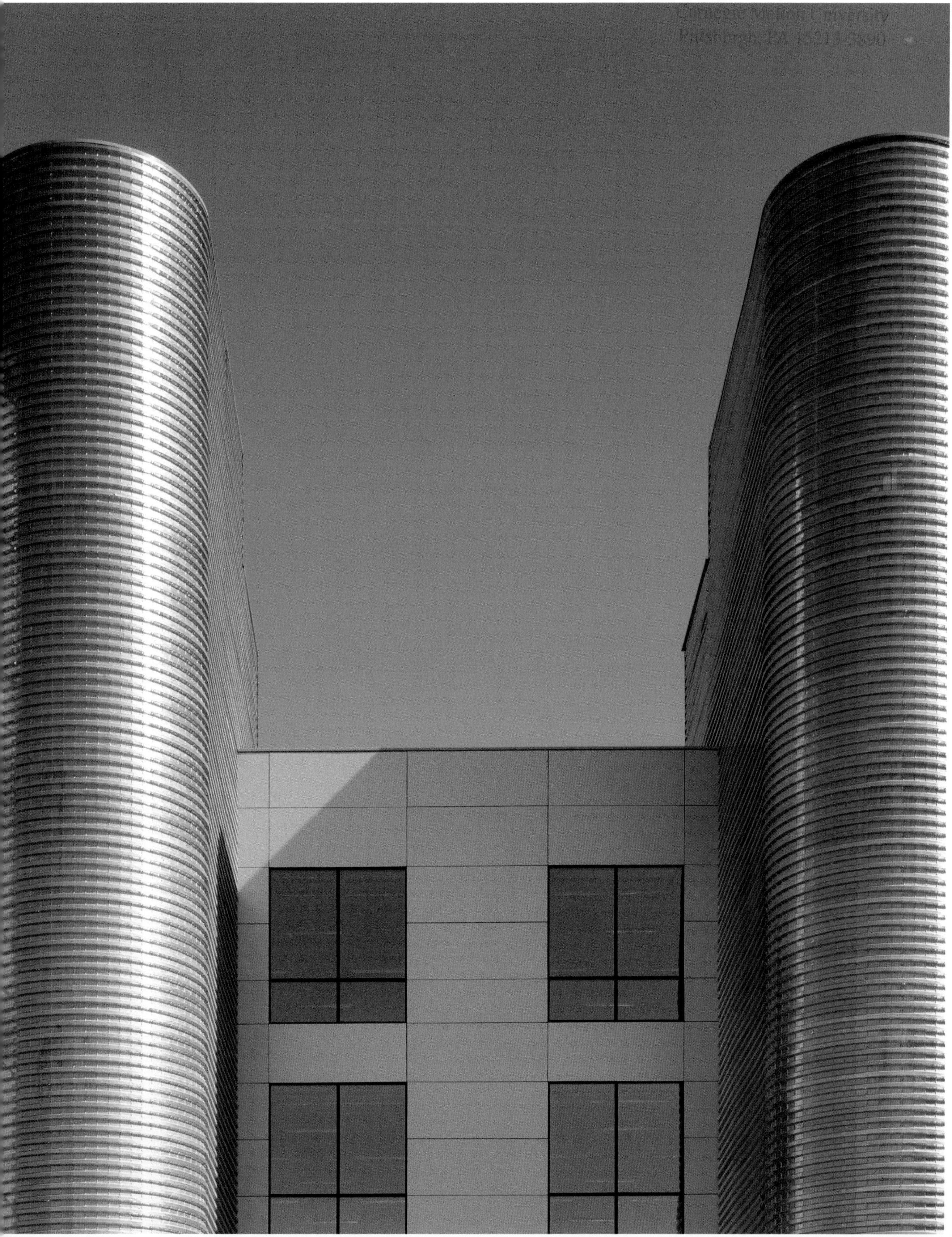

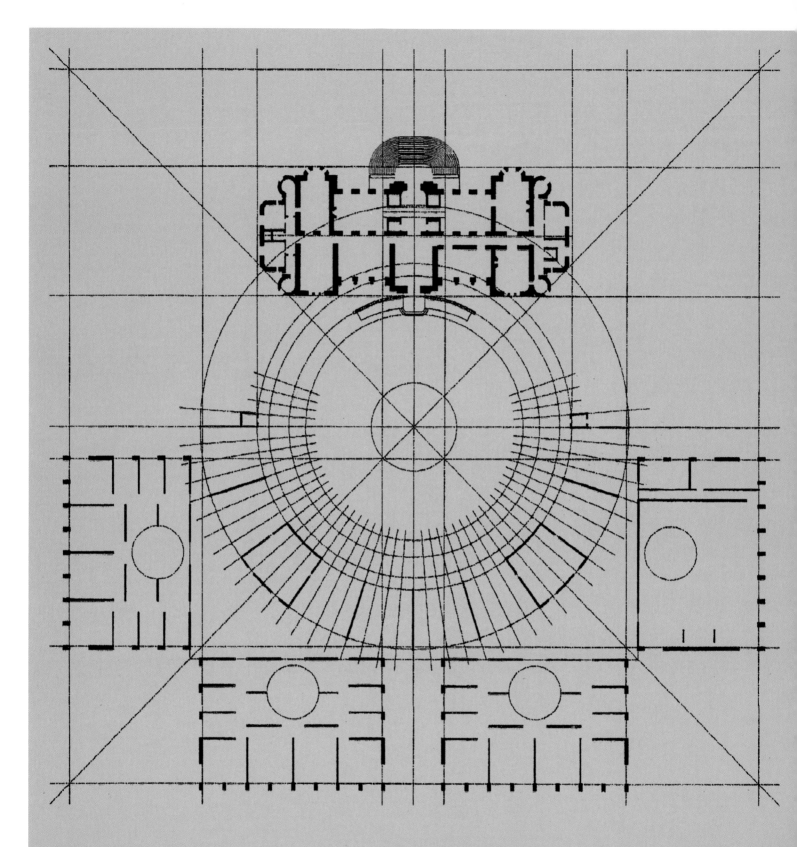

# A Discourse on Method

■ Denis Valode and Jean Pistre don't resemble many other successful architects. They are both soft-spoken, and in a time when inflated egos dominate their profession, they share an office and seem to rarely disagree. Valode was born in Charenton-le-Pont in 1946 and Pistre in Nice in 1951. They both attended the UPI (which is today called the *École d'architecture Paris-Villemin*) and they created their own firm in 1977. In the curious world of French architecture where public and private sector projects rarely are undertaken by the same firms, they have specialized in buildings designed for promoters and large companies, although there are some notable exceptions to this rule in their body of work. The spacious, bright offices of Valode & Pistre, located on the rue de Bac in the 7th arrondissement of Paris, give an impression of clarity and calm that actually gives quite an accurate idea of their architecture. Although they have begun to build in numerous countries, from Mexico to China, they have avoided the kind of excessive rhetoric that often seems to accompany "star" architects. Indeed, Denis Valode and Jean Pistre are not "stars" in their behavior or design, rather they are intent on being original and making their buildings work both for the clients and for the ultimate users.

Valode & Pistre do, in fact, have a style, but this style is not readily apparent in their structures because of the time and effort put into making each building correspond to its setting and to its use. Their work is modern, but not Modernist because they willingly appropriate or renovate existing structures and always respond to context. They are computer literate but not committed to full digital design. Denis Valode in particular is a skilled draughtsman and his sketches often explain projects better than a DVD full of computer drawings. The culture of modesty that they seem to have given to their practice does not rule out spectacular, innovative buildings like the L'Oréal factory in Aulnay-sous-Bois, but it does allow talent from within the office to express itself in unexpected ways. Thus a recent project, the Hyatt Hotel for Ekaterinburg in Russia was designed not by the principals, but by a young architect, Valérie Vaconsin who won one of the regular in-house competitions. Quite far removed from the *tabula rasa* of Bauhaus Modernism, Valode & Pistre have actively sought out links between their projects and science, ethnology, art, sociology or history. And although there is virtue in all of these facts, they do not seek to proclaim a brave new world for architecture as much as they work patiently in a way that seems natural to them. Rather than an isolated object, a building by Valode & Pistre is conceived as being part of a tissue of relationships and situations. They examine location, activity and history and then propose solutions that may be very unexpected, but remain the fruit of their analysis of the precise situation involved. When they designed the generic factories for the Valéo group, the architects wove a certain number of obvious needs into their charter. Daylight and openings to the exterior were essential, and truck traffic was never to cross a pedestrian path. In a way these ideas are so obvious as to escape the domain of architecture and to approach that of psychology or physiology, and yet this is how Valode & Pistre assemble their own vision of modernity. The technical aspects of architecture and engineering also fascinate them. Their Hall 4 for the Paris-Expo site is 250 meters long, by 84 meters wide with a clear interior height of 10.5 meters. Beams spanning the full 84-meter width generate a spectacular, column free space which is at the heart of the architectural design, and yet its realization is technically inspired and gives results that make the exhibition activity planned for the building much easier to organize than in comparable structures.

## Art: From Old Bricks to the Avant-Garde

An early and untypical project of Valode & Pistre that shows a good number of their qualities is their renovation of the *Centre d'arts plastiques contemporain* in Bordeaux (Capc). Built in 1824 near the Garonne River, close to the center of Bordeaux, the *Entrepôt réel des denrées colonials*, or Entrepôt Lainé was intended to stock spices, chocolate and vanilla coming from the French colonies. Built of brick, Bourg stone and Oregon red pine, it was an intentionally heavy and dark structure, meant to protect its contents from the heat and light of the sun. Laid out in an orthogonal plan, the warehouse fits into a site in the form of an irregular pentagon, and was not an obvious choice for the exhibition of contemporary art. That was however, between 1978 and 1991 what Mayor Jacques Chaban-Delmas and Capc director Jean-

Louis Froment turned it into with the able assistance of Valode & Pistre. Although he started out with a more noble structure, their effort was similar to that undertaken by the Italian architect Andrea Bruno at the Castello di Rivoli in Turin.

Rivoli was built in fits and starts by the Savoy family beginning in the early 17th century on the site of a medieval castle above Turin. A 1718 plan by Filippo Juvara to renovate the castle was halted one-third of the way through. Abandoned or used as troop barracks until the 20th century, the building was studied by Andrea Bruno beginning in the 1960's and he proposed a plan to restore it without any "modern" intervention except where necessary. It was not until 1984 that the first exhibition of contemporary art was held there. The Castello di Rivoli shares with the Capc an essentially brick structure, a program of exhibition for contemporary art, and sensitive, historically aware restorations. Both Andrea Bruno and Valode & Pistre were well ahead of their times in proposing such audaciously modest plans.

The Entrepôt was designed by the engineer Claude Deschamps and built in a period of 21 months between 1822 and 1824. It may have been that Goya, at the time exiled in Bordeaux attended its inauguration. Although it is decidedly austere in its appearance, the structure has been compared to that of a caravanserai or a basilica. Abandoned and then purchased by the city of Bordeaux, the Entrepôt was listed as a historic monument in 1973. In 1974, Patrick Mazery and Jean Pistre proposed to convert the building into a cultural center. One year later, the city decided on a complete renovation to be carried out by Michel Joanne and two young associate architects, Denis Valode and Jean Pistre. A first, largely technical intervention was carried out in 1979 and permitted the installation in the building of the Sigma theater festival and a gallery for the Capc. In 1984, the decorator Andrée Putman was associated in a second phase where the central gallery, eleven exhibition spaces, a library, café and educational service were created. A final phase of the work began in 1989, where the central volume, or *Grande Nef* as it is called was restored to its original form, and 3,000 m² of extra exhibition and library space were completed. The Capc and the smaller *Arc-en-rêve centre d'architecture* now would occupy the entire building.

Perhaps one of the most significant aspects of the intervention of Valode & Pistre on the Entrepôt Lainé is in fact their modesty. While they could have made a case for a much more apparent intervention, and self-consciously attempted to erase all traces of the past inside this great old structure, they chose not only to live with what was there, but to place it in evidence so that visitors could experience something that no completely modern building can transmit — a sense of time. Modesty also is apparent in the idea of economy that is apparent in many of their projects. They don't seek to fill their buildings with cheap materials to make a point like some illustrious internationally known architects, but they search for the inherent efficiency of a project and make it economical by creating a maximal effect with limited means. As Denis Valode says, "I have noted the work of the Japanese architect Shuhei Endo who creates curved structures in corrugated metal. His forms are in fact completely logical and he doesn't need a hundred computers to calculate their design. We are convinced that the role of the architect is to do more with less and not the contrary. The economy of means — the correct choice of means — is essential. Putting gigantic means into play for a tiny result is not in the logic of construction nor of architecture. Our goal is to create the best possible result with a certain economy of means."

Like Andrea Bruno at Rivoli, Valode & Pistre showed an exceptional attachment to a single project, in Bordeaux carrying it forward over a period of more than a decade. They also succeeded in carefully restoring unusual historic buildings, leaving intact the spirit of the structures and making their own additions clearly different from the work of the past. Rivoli is a heavy building, if not as dark as the Entrepôt Lainé, but both architects have turned these unlikely remnants from other eras into convincing spaces dedicated to the most contemporary art.

A number of other early projects of Valode & Pistre confirm the nature of their specific methods. Their Bélier Foundry in Verac (1978-79) was a design selected in a competition organized by the French National Agency for the Improvement of Working Conditions (*Agence Nationale pour l'amélioration des conditions de travail*). They engaged in lengthy discussions with both workers and administrative personnel as well as specialists such as a sociologist before proposing an architectural solution. As it happens, a number of the ideas they later developed for Valéo and others, such as an axial arrangement and a specificity in the usage of given spaces are present in this early project. Long interested in the rapport between art and architecture, they called on Speedy Graphito to create bright, colorful wall paintings for a school in Paris (1988-90). As the architects explain, "Turning away from static exhibitions, galleries or museums, contemporary artists are exploring questions of context and relationship with place. Spatial projection and organization is increasingly present in artistic creation. While our work as architects differs fundamentally from that of the artist, being subject to functional, social and legal constraints, there are overlapping fields of interest. This complicity provides a possibility for mutual enrichment... Each actor remains in his or her domain without seeking to mimic the other. Architecture design has no interest in reproducing a *déjà vu* formalism, while the artist is free to modify, enrich and transform a context adhering to his own intellectual process. Artists offer a different point of view on the world and on our work." Though this commentary may at first seem somewhat distant from the consultative process launched by Valode & Pistre in Verac, it is in fact a manifestation of the same attitude: an openness and a willingness to allow others to contribute to the success of a building.

Nor is the rapport with artists a superficial one for the architects. They have called on a number of different types of artists both in their projects, as was the case in their Leonardo da Vinci University (Courbevoie, 1992-95) where works of the painters Jean-Charles

Blais and Aki Kuroda grace the windows and the walls, and in their own offices, where artists such as Felice Varini have created temporary installations. One of their current projects, the Beaugrenelle shopping center in Paris, will have exterior wall designs conceived by the Swiss artist Rémy Zaugg who has frequently worked with Herzog & de Meuron. There appears to be a continuity in the choice of the artists who intervene at the invitation of Valode & Pistre – they are decidedly modern in their spirit but not necessarily abstract. Where some contemporary artists could create bewildering or aggressive works, the architects apparently seek a relationship with their own work that is fundamentally modern but humane. Again, Valode & Pistre seek a clear and simple solution even for complex problems. Admitting that people who use their buildings are sensitive not only to architecture but to a series of other factors Valode & Pistre make consultation and enrichment part of their process – part of what finally has become their own "style."

## Cars: From Design to Spare Parts

Despite their very real unpretentiousness, Denis Valode and Jean Pistre have long since proven their ability to handle very large-scale projects. One of the most ambitious of these, even if they were not the architects of the entire complex was the Renault Technocentre located in Guyancourt. Chosen over Architecture-Studio, Alain Sarfati, and Jean-Paul Viguier as the result of a competition organized by the automobile manufacturer, Valode & Pistre laid out the master plan for a complex measuring 146 hectares with an original total of 363,000 m$^2$ of floor area developed for some 6,300 employees. "The program called for a type of city of research," says Denis Valode. "We based our concept on an urban plan that had the capacity to evolve over time. The goal of Renault was to be able to design a car in one year instead of the six required previously by bringing together all of the services that are involved in this process. The construction process produced vast quantities of earth, and we used these to create a bucolic environment, with wooded hills that look as though they had always

been there." The proximity of industrial facilities to nature, if only in the form of a limited garden, is a constant in the work of the firm, and in Guyancourt they were working on such a vast scale that they were able to manufacture a "natural" landscape for the complex. Aside from building two major structures, La Ruche (the Beehive, completed in 1997) and Le Gradient, completed in 2003, Valode & Pistre participated in the jury selection of other architects who worked on the Technocentre. La Ruche is almost like a city in itself, with its 142,000 m$^2$ of floor area and offices for 3,500 employees. The orthogonal layout of the full complex certainly gives a hint of modernity that is confirmed by the architecture, including that of such groups as Chaix & Morel. "Is the Technocentre modernist, or is it based on Chinese, Spanish or Roman cities? The goal was to reunite the activities of Renault. The real challenge was to make the different services communicate properly. We created an orthogonal system because it is easier to understand where one is. There are all kinds of passageways within the complex that improve the speed of contact of the team," he concludes. Renault selected the master plan of Valode & Pistre because of their good relations with the architects, but they also cited "the reasonable fees requested by the architects, their attention to quality, cost and deadlines." The automobile manufacturer also appreciated that the master plan takes into account the main phases in the conception of a vehicle, and that the architects succeeded in "placing the Technocentre on an urban line that runs from the bell tower of the city's church to the farm of Villaroy." In other words despite the relative self-sufficiency of the complex, the architects nonetheless took into account what was around them and what goes on inside the Technocentre from the first moment. The orthogonal modernity of the plan is undeniable, but so too is the fact that it is rooted in realities that go beyond the strict realm of architecture, entering into historical and technical considerations, while creating the proper conditions for the sort of active communication between its employees that Renault was clearly looking for. Obviously the result of an intensive dialogue with the company, the Technocentre is also the fruit of an understated vision of architecture, one that roots the buildings in the earth rather than perching them on alien soil.

The managers of the French-based global car parts manufacturer Valéo have a high opinion of architecture. As they have written in their 2003 *Factory Design* handbook, "Architecture is a component of productivity and quality, contributing to create a work environment in which Valéo employees can develop their skills and the Valéo production system can be fully implemented." About the publication itself, they write, "Today, the *Valéo Factory Design* handbook presents a comprehensive approach for all aspects of construction or refurbishment of a Valéo plant, covers: project management; function and architecture; regulations and performance specifications; contract specifications." The essentials of this plan were laid out not by specialists in manufacturing processes but by Valode & Pistre. "We respect the process of production," says Denis Valode, "but we don't start with that. We have decided long since that certain elements like the fact that trucks must not cross pedestrian passageways are not negotiable. We engage in a project with the goal of creating a synthesis of the needs of the client, the workers, and the industrial process, as well as taking into account specific local cultural elements. If we privilege one factor over the others, we inevitably create a bad project. Dialogue is of great interest to us, but we engage in it in a didactic mode. How can certain problems that arise in the production process be resolved? There is no such thing as geometric truth where process is concerned."

The touch of Valode & Pistre is frequently obvious in the *Valéo Factory Design* handbook. Where landscaping is concerned, for example, Valéo writes, "Landscape design should demonstrate that Valéo industrial activities are developed in full harmony with the natural environment." In the plans offered by the firm, restaurants, employees' areas and plant management are in contiguous zones located on one side of the factory. Where "Natural light and views to the exterior" are concerned, the handbook states, "Windows provide additional daylight, but more importantly open views to the outdoors and create an important psychological link with the exterior for production workers... It is necessary... to provide visual contact with the exterior to humanize the work environment."

Valode & Pistre have thus far undertaken eight factory projects themselves in San Luis Potosi, Mexico; Skawina, Poland; Zebrak, Czech Republic; Utique, Tunisia; Bouznika, Morocco; Gezbe, Turkey; Veszprem, Hungary; and Chrzanow, Poland. At least eight other architects, such as Ackermann und Partner in Germany or Noriaki Okabe Architecture Network S.A. in Japan have also built factories for Valéo using the Valode & Pistre program. The fact that both architects and Valéo accept this situation and continue to base their factory construction program on the Valode & Pistre model is a clear tribute to the work of the Parisians. Some might consider the time and effort that the architects put into the original factory design superfluous, but to Valode & Pistre, it is the heart of their effort, going well beyond traditional architectural problems to deal with factors such as the well-being of workers. Though, on reflection, such considerations obviously have a direct bearing on the success of the architecture, they are rarely listed amongst the priorities of architects, especially the well-known sort. It seems apparent in the case of Valéo that the investment in time and effort made by the architects at the outset of the process has been amply returned in that they have been involved themselves in eight factory projects.

## Towers: Site and Identity

Valode & Pistre have quite a number of tall buildings in their project list and this is surely no accident. Rather than treating structures 100 to 200 meters tall as isolated objects, they have successfully sought to integrate them into their urban environments. As usual, this is not simply a matter of a nice shape; it also has to do with the overall design of the buildings, both internal and exterior. One of their most poetic designs is for the current T1 project at La Défense in Paris. The architects' presentation of this structure reveals something about their design process and the thinking that goes into their buildings. The firm's brochure for T1 compares its shape successively to that of the sail of an America's Cup yacht, the Flatiron Building in Manhattan and a snow-covered mountain peak. "Seen from the south and the heart of La Défense," they write, "T1 will appear to come forward to meet the viewer like the bow of a great ship. Seen from the east and west, the tower's sail-like profile cuts across the landscape. Seen from the north, the progressively curved façade suggests a great stairway or mountain side 'disappearing' into the sky." "The tower forms a street angle, so we compared it to the Flatiron Building," explains Denis Valode. "It's like a great sheet of paper folded at the street angle. But as for the rounded edge, we are fans of Jean Prouvé, who never made angle joints, there is a continuity in the building surface that way. The rounding also helps the tower to fit in more smoothly. In architecture, it is essential to always have more than one reason for a decision. A series of concomitant reasons are necessary to find a pertinent solution."

The architects offer computer views showing how the 190-meter bulk of the structure will in fact fit in quite well with the view from across the Seine. This is partially due to the curved form of the back of the tower evoked in their description. What seems esthetically pleasing from various angles is in fact the result of a simple calculation: to create office floors with a minimum net usable area of approximately 1,300 m² they have taken into account that the upper levels require less mechanical (elevator) space than the lower ones. In fact, Valode & Pistre were obliged to slightly redesign the building in late 2001 to increase the available floor space on the upper levels. It seems that their esthetic image of the tower made it even more elegant than the clients wished, but Valode & Pistre found a solution that both meets the clients' needs and retains the distinctive silhouette of T1. Set at the edge of La Défense, the building also is meant to have an urban function denied to many towers that

simply rise out of the concrete without taking into account anything other than their own entrance. "It marks the entrance to Courbevoie," says Valode. "The tower and the second building required by the plan form a round square. A street, a boulevard and a square meet here. We wanted to create a public space the way architects always have. Curiously though, the height of the building was imposed on us, but not the creation of the square. It is very French to impose building heights in such a strict way, whereas American cities are much more variable in their height restrictions."

The five towers being designed by the architects for a site in Beijing take into account the site and cultural preoccupations in quite different ways than T1. Aware that the Chinese are at once proud of their cultural heritage and wary of foreigners who propose a "Chinese-style" building, they took to studying calligraphy and more specifically the stone blocks used to print certain texts. Without going so far as to use actual ideograms they nonetheless inspired themselves from these blocks to create a floating stone façade whose openings do bring to mind Chinese characters albeit in an abstract way. Most recent construction in Beijing is heavily clad in stone. The French architects have bowed to this esthetic preference while retaining the lightness that is more their strength, detaching the stone façade from the inner glass core of the towers. They have also taken into account the encounter of diagonal and north-south orthogonal street patterns that meet at the site to make their project an obvious part of this particular location in the Chinese capital. Finally, they refer to the famous Five Pagoda Temple, a site in Beijing, without belaboring the comparison or giving the impression that they are in any sense engaging in a historic pastiche. Treading on particularly sensitive territory, where a number of other western architects appear to have committed stylistic *faux pas*, Valode & Pistre have proposed a typically subtle combination of the various influences that play on the site and the buildings they have been called on to design. Where others such as their French colleague Paul Andreu or the Dutch architect Rem

Koolhaas (OMA) have designed dramatic geometric or computer inspired forms for Beijing, Valode & Pistre have stayed in a more expected rectangular mode for their towers, and sought to pay some homage to the great culture of the country they are working in. The Jiuxianqiao complex demonstrates that the observational methods and sensitivity that have served the architects particularly well in France can indeed be translated onto foreign ground.

## The Versailles Instinct: Havas Headquarters and Cap Gemini / Ernst & Young University

On more than one occasion, Valode & Pistre have been confronted with an older building located on one of their sites. Whereas a typical Modernist response might be to want to demolish such a structure in order to give fullest importance to the new design, the architects have consistently opted for the preservation of such vestiges of the past. This clearly has to do with more firmly implanting their own architecture in a historic setting, giving it a legitimacy of place that would otherwise be difficult to acquire. A first case of this nature is the Havas headquarters in Suresnes developed for Hines. Jean Barot built the Coty factory in 1939 in a distinctively modern style, using brick, concrete and glass. Hines describes the challenge posed by this site as being "threefold: past, present and future." As they write, "The past meant Suresnes and was embodied in the former Coty perfume factory, still standing as a vestige of the town's architectural heritage. Valode & Pistre opted for fidelity and continuity. They kept the former factory, which included workshops, offices and a boiler room. The layout of the three new additions to the building employs meticulous geometry so subtly that the resulting structure is immediately striking in its obvious and harmonious unity." Denis Valode explains that the architects were entirely free to demolish the older building if they wished. "What is important is a way of looking at the site, including what we decided to preserve of the 1930's building. It was in good condition, but all along the Seine, similar structures have been demolished

in recent years. We wanted to implicate ourselves in a vision of what existed in the past. We wanted to spotlight the quality and interest of the older building while creating an extremely modern structure behind it. The use of brick in the newer building underlines the continuity." The architects' particular interest for older architecture is revealed in Denis Valode's comments about one aspect of the Coty building – its fine concrete window structure near the former boiler room. "We wanted to redo the window, but current regulations make such fine concrete window frames impossible to recreate. We wound up restoring the window and putting a protective sheet of glass behind it."

While Denis Valode compares the Havas project to the construction of Versailles where Louis XIV. specifically requested the preservation of an existing hunting pavilion at the heart of the new building, a second complex, designed by Valode & Pistre has almost more relation to this instinct than does the Havas building. Their corporate university campus for Cap Gemini / Ernst & Young University located in Gouvieux, near Chantilly outside of Paris makes full use of a Rothschild castle that they had the option to demolish. Rather, they chose to undertake a painstaking renovation of the eclectic late-19th century structure, which included the complete reconstruction of one wing, and they made the castle the heart of their design for the forward-looking international consultancy and accounting firm. The main, semi-circular structures they designed for the client are turned toward the front of the castle and aligned on its center. Clearly, this plan was attractive to the clients who wished to emphasize the French ownership of the group. For Cap Gemini and many others, the very symbolism of France is less its undeniable modernity but rather its cultural wealth and its historic monuments. Had the Rothschild castle been torn down, it is clear that the corporate university could have been located anywhere in the world, but this was not at all the intention of the clients. Keeping and indeed restoring the existing building was the most obvious way to affirm the roots of the site and therefore of the firm itself. Working like "architects from the historic preservation authority" Valode & Pistre took obvious pleasure and interest in bringing what was almost a ruin back to its pristine, original condition. They also studied the work of Edwin Lutyens, erstwhile reference point of Post-Modern architects, to see how he had handled his own work on historic English residences. As they write, "The composition that results from the interaction of the semi-circular new buildings with the castle is inspired by the work of Lutyens in Great Britain, which was contemporary with the construction of the Rothschild castle, using the themes of the winter garden, the circle and a strongly axial layout." Although Valode rather unexpectedly compares the style of the old building to "Disneyland architecture," because of its varied sources, the architects wrote that, "The eclectic style of the architect of the castle, Félix Langlais was a real opportunity. His multiple points of reference (Louis XIII., Middle Ages etc), his sense of humor (the exaggerated tips of the small towers on the castle), gave us a great deal of liberty in creating our own set of relationships between the past, present and future. His open spirit freed ours." Although they worked with a landscape architect, Valode & Pistre themselves have always had a strong interest in gardens. In the case of the Cap Gemini / Ernst & Young campus, they laid out the half-circle opposite the castle like a "sundial, with potted plants indicating the hours," thus recalling the days of company employees attending the university "with their rhythm of study, relaxation or meals, like ancient monasteries, guardians of knowledge and places of learning."

## Breathing Life into Old Bricks, Timber and Concrete – from Bercy Village to La Défense

A theory made popular by a well-known architect would have it that all construction, from museums to urbanism is fundamentally influenced by the logic of shopping. At a time when covered shopping centers have made their inroads throughout the world, islands of commerce unto themselves, it may be difficult to maintain that there is not some truth in this idea.

Confronted with a site at the eastern Paris that had long been used as the city's wine storage area, Valode & Pistre, as has often been the case, opted for the preservation and renovation of the existing wine warehouses as the heart of a new shopping center. These are not vast spaces like the Entrepôt Lainé in Bordeaux, but rather small and low, and as such presumably not ideal for commerce. Another standard assumption of such projects would be that the passageways between stores should be covered for use in bad weather, but Valode & Pistre opted not only for the preservation of the existing façades but they kept the open street running perpendicularly to the Seine between the warehouse buildings. They erected bands of larger modern buildings parallel to the original structures, using a zigzag pattern for the roofs that recalls the early covered markets of Paris, and they necessarily allowed for planned passages from the neighboring park through the Bercy Village complex. Any visitor, especially on weekends, can see the tangible proof of the success of this concept. Crowds fill the space, and readily use the theoretically cramped boutiques along the central street to full capacity. Making their restoration or reconstruction of the warehouses visible as a modern intervention, Valode & Pistre have managed to preserve the historic interest of this space, without tuning into a Disney experience, no small feat. The juxtaposition of old and new successfully integrated into the Bercy Village complex has seen a more recent addition, the 18-movie theater UGC Bercy Ciné-Cité also created by Valode & Pistre. Replacing an originally planned office building on a site that sits astride the Cours St. Emilion at the Seine River side of Bercy Village, the movie theaters of course add to the number of persons who frequent the shops, but the architects have also made an urban statement with their building. Axially arranged so that a central atrium slices through the Ciné-Cité in the direction of the Seine, the building affirms that vestiges of the old city and indeed its fundamental urban realities are not at all incompatible with modernity. Given the numerous heavy-handed attempts to develop Paris along the Seine River that have occurred in the past, for example at the Front de Seine, the success of Valode & Pistre is a considerable accomplishment. This is not "signature" architecture, but modest, efficient work for the real world. It is modest in the sense that the architects have seen the virtue of leaving the traces of the past on a site, anchoring it to its history, giving it a legitimacy that an entirely new building could not have. It is efficient because it works – it brings in people who want to come back, and who spend money while they are there. No amount of theory can achieve such a result, it requires a sense of the city and of what people want.

Glasgow in Scotland is so far north that its winters are longer and darker than those of most of Europe. This could very easily be a depressing place, and indeed, with the decline of its traditional industries like shipbuilding, the city suffered a long and difficult period of decline in the 20th century. And yet Glasgow is also a center of culture, home to Charles Rennie Mackintosh (1868-1928), and more recently a city that has seen exciting new buildings like Norman Foster's Scottish Exhibition and Conference Centre (SECC), a £30 million 3,000 seat facility intended to complement the existing center. They rise along the banks of the Clyde. The city's interest in design and architecture is further demonstrated by the existence of The Lighthouse, a 1999 conversion of Mackintosh's 1895 Glasgow Herald newspaper office. The center's "vision is to develop the links between design, architecture and the creative industries, seeing these as interconnected social, educational, economic and cultural issues of concern to everyone." Since opening The Lighthouse has welcomed well over one million visitors. Despite the strong presence of Mackintosh in Glasgow, Jean Pistre says quite simply that he did not look to the famous Glaswegian in designing his vast new project for the former Graving Dock area. "A main concern was the low light in winter," says the French architect, "so there is plenty of glass." Although Valode & Pistre make specific references to buildings such as the Flatiron in New York, or architects like Edwin Lutyens, their architecture is not one of appropriation or imitation. It is typical of them not to look specifically to Mackintosh in these circum-

stances, since he would have been the most obvious, or "easiest" reference in Glasgow. Their work certainly fits in with many modern designs, but it does not appear to be derivative because their sources are more rarely prestigious colleagues than they are the imperatives of a site or a project. On their site in Glasgow, there is above all what remains of one of Europe's premier shipping yards, the elaborate timber dry docks that warranted a listing "as buildings of special architectural or historic interest of the highest category (A)" pronounced on May 15, 1987. Though they are physically imposing and impressive, the Graving Docks are also an incarnation of the real working history of Glasgow, not the upper-end design of a Mackintosh but the logical trace of 19th century industry. The preservation of industrial sites has of course become quite popular, and locations from Bordeaux's Entrepôt Lainé to England's own Baltic Centre for Contemporary Arts (Newcastle, 1999-2002) created by Dominic Williams in the former Baltic Flour Mills building, but in Glasgow, the Graving Dock represents something of the very life-blood of the city and Valode & Pistre were clearly sensitive to this. Despite the listing it would have been possible for the French architects, together with their local partners to build over the dock site. Rather they have chosen, typically, to retain and restore one of the facilities, dock 2. They have further sought to design their buildings in a ship-like configuration, which is of course logical for this location and in keeping with much of the tradition of modern architecture, from Louis Sullivan on. Again, a mixture of respect for the historic interest of a site, even one far removed in this case from their personal experience, and a talent for designing attractive modern buildings that do not deny their location, characterize Valode & Pistre more than any stylistic or theoretical rhetoric.

Back in Paris, the architects are dealing with a bit of the city's history that is much less rich and interesting than either the Bercy wine warehouses or Graving Dock. French President Georges Pompidou and his successor Valéry Giscard d'Estaing had different ideas about how to design the city best. The centralized system in France is rare amongst democracies in that it actually allows presidents to play a role in such decisions, left elsewhere to specialists or the free marketplace. Pompidou's grand visions of modernity gave Paris La Défense, the Tour Montparnasse and the Front de Seine area, none of which can be termed successful in the urban sense, or in the architectural sense. Inspired by American cities, presumably provincial ones, the French went on a modern building spree in the late 1960s and early 1970s that culminated in the construction of the Centre Georges Pompidou (Piano & Rogers, 1977). The Front de Seine in the 15th arrondissement of Paris along the banks of the Seine is dotted with a mixed bag of 94-meter high apartment buildings and office towers and hotels. The Beaugrenelle shopping center, in the midst of this high-rise neighborhood was originally meant to be a real experiment in modernity, separating pedestrian and vehicular traffic and allowing residents to accede directly to the stores from an upper level platform. Unfortunately Valéry Giscard d'Estaing, who had a taste more for the picturesque than the modern in architecture intervened in the process and succeeded only in derailing the original plan, creating a heterogeneous, soulless place that has fallen in recent years into a time of declining sales and clientele. Taking on a modern nightmare like Beaugrenelle and turning it into a going concern that brightens its neighborhood instead of making it even more depressing is just the kind of task that Valode & Pistre seem to enjoy. Some might have said that the whole complex should be demolished, but working with promoters Apsys and Gécina, they have come up with a scheme that returns order and commercial sense to Beaugrenelle. With visible entrances, a strong diagonal axis and a wrap-around glass skin, the architects give unity back to the center. By daring to slice through a thick concrete slab covering one street running perpendicularly to the Seine, they have given value to the street-level boutiques that should always have been prime locations but here never were. Finally, in a bit of daring that in some ways goes even beyond their purely architectural gestures, Valode & Pistre have called on the Swiss artist Rémy Zaugg to

help to give a cultural aspect to Beaugrenelle that surely was not part of its original make-up. Zaugg is a bit of a hard-liner, working frequently with the neon-obsessed team from Herzog & de Meuron, but he is as close to avant-garde as one can come in the limited field where art and architecture meet.

How can a building that is of the modern period and yet outdated and unusable be turned into a shining example of the most contemporary architecture? This was the challenge that Valode & Pistre faced with their PB12 project in La Défense. Built in 1970, the Crédit Lyonnais tower was an outstanding example of the heavy-handed modernism that dominated the period in Paris. Relatively small usable surfaces (800 m² per floor), an overly dense load-bearing façade with pillars located every 1.4 meters, and a symmetric design that made finding the entrance a hard task, and large areas below grade without natural lighting, were the essential problems of the structure. Having ruled out demolition and wanting to keep the existing floor area, the owner of the tower, the insurance company AXA, called on Valode & Pistre not just to solve the problems but to turn the PB12 tower into a statement of the firm's commitment to quality in architecture. The finished structure shows none of the extraordinary process required for the architects to perform this almost miraculous conversion. They opted for a complete replacement of the original façade with a new, contemporary design. In order to accomplish this, they erected a structural shell around the old building, driving beams into the central core to hold it up as they demolished the original load-bearing face from the top down. Adding 200 m² per floor in the process, they recovered usable floor area from the underground space by creating an atrium that brings daylight into the lower levels, making them more valuable and usable than they were. A clearly marked entrance related to this atrium completes a process that is surely architectural, but is also strongly a feat of engineering. The result was slightly more expensive than a new construction, but avoided the considerable costs and other risks that would have been created by a decision to demolish the old building. With

1,000 m² per floor, the new PB12 tower meets the most rigorous international standards for office space and certainly satisfies AXA's stringent quality demands. Though the original Crédit Lyonnais tower has disappeared entirely in this process, it remains at the core of the PB12 building. This is certainly not a renovation in the traditional sense of the word, but it does have some similarity to the Beaugrenelle project in which the architects have transported a modern but unusable core into the 21ˢᵗ century.

## To the Ends of Europe and Beyond

Valode & Pistre are currently engaged in projects at both the eastern and western end of Europe, in different contexts, but with equally modern ambitions. In Madrid, near the Barajas Airport they have developed a business park concept (Las Mercedes) that takes into account the roadside site by creating an internal garden, freed from cars by underground parking. They create independent office units that can function separately at the same time as they share some common spaces and an overall design coherence that means they also fit together. Here, the site dictates a more or less closed external periphery while the architects' own insistence with the quality of working conditions harmonizes well with the idea of the central garden, visible from a maximum possible number of offices. Umbrella-like structures serve to shield the buildings from the intense summer heat confirming the architects' desire to make a humane and efficient addition to the architectural alternatives on offer in the Spanish capital.

Where heat is the main problem in Madrid, holding the cold at bay is the issue in Valode & Pistre's Hyatt Hotel for Ekaterinburg in Russia, designed as a result of an in-house competition by one of the young architects in their office. Ekaterinburg is known as the place where the former Czar Nicholas II., his wife Alexandra, their four daughters and Czarevitch Alexis were killed by the Bolsheviks on July 16, 1918. It is precisely on the location of the Ipatiev House where they were assassinated that the *Cathedral-on-the-Blood* or

*Cathedral of the Martyrs of Russia* was built and inaugurated on July 16, 2003, 85 years after the events. It is of course no accident that the outstanding hotel being erected by Valode & Pistre will be turned directly toward the axis of the Cathedral. As a symbolic center of civic pride, the Cathedral is built in an ample, traditional style, while the Hyatt Hotel will of course be much more contemporary in its architecture. The sensitivity shown by the architects to local culture and environment has led them to work on other projects for the city that stands astride the limit between Asia and Europe.

These last two projects are symbolic of the geographic reach of the office of Valode & Pistre even if they have gone on to China with other work. It might not be obvious to the simple visitor that the same architects are responsible for the renovation of the CAPC in Bordeaux and the Hyatt Hotel in Ekaterinburg. External stylistic elements are surely not a good guide to understanding what underlies the very real relationship of these projects. It has become clear that the real style of Denis Valode, Jean Pistre and their office is a coherent and intelligent way of looking at each new building. The very basic questions that many well-known architects fail to ever ask are at the very heart of their method: What is the goal of the building, what is its history, what are the structural solutions that are best adopted to the problems posed? These and other questions have allowed Valode & Pistre to develop an extremely impressive body of work in a relatively short period of time. In a sense their career has been made by their capacity to ask and to respond to the most obvious questions. They have eschewed a dogmatic approach, indulging even in the painstaking reconstruction of an eclectic late-19ᵗʰ century castle for example. But they have never crossed the line into pastiche, even when they were rebuilding the wine warehouses of Bercy, they did so as part of an overall modern concept. That they have branched out well beyond the borders of France, is a tribute to their methods rather than to any overweaning ambition. Although 200-meter high towers are not a priori modest buildings, there is a fundamental unpretentiousness to the work of Valode & Pistre. Their L'Oréal Factory is anything but dull. Calling on the most sophisticated engineering capacities of the moment, it is exciting and bright. If it is biomorphic, the L'Oréal Factory appears as an exception in this respect in the oeuvre of the architects. They are interested in art, but do not take themselves for artists, even if they make excellent drawings. They are interested in engineering, but in cooperation with people like the late Peter Rice or their own engineering staff. They delight in references from icy mountain peaks to Versailles, but their work is in no sense an imitation of any of these forms. The references are a part of their thought process and a way of explaining their ideas to clients who may not be overly familiar with the technical aspects of architecture.

An overview of the work of Valode & Pistre begins and ends in the same place, the office the two architects share overlooking the rue du Bac in Paris. Many architectural partnerships have been dissolved over questions of ego and differing styles, but Denis Valode and Jean Pistre share more than an office – they share a way of looking at things and a capacity to set aside differences and to allow each other full expression. It may be that Denis Valode speaks more easily than his partner, but both have left their mark on the work that they sign in common. As much as anything, the real style of the firm must be an expression of their characters, representing the best of what the French call their "Cartesian" character, solving problems in a pragmatic and efficient way, setting aside conflict and the superficial in favor of an in-depth analysis of each project. Although it is difficult to judge internal office relationships, especially where more than 100 persons are concerned, it also seems that Denis Valode and Jean Pistre are benevolent and open in their relations with their *équipe*, something of a rarity in a country that is still given to frequent displays of outmoded paternalism. They have clearly managed to profit from ongoing relationships with powerful promoters or other clients, who have been impressed by their sense of continuity and stability. Thus, their perseverance and talent will lead them to eventually give

a completely new form to the main exhibition park of Paris. So too, the projects that they have carried out for promoters on a speculative basis, have become the proud headquarters of substantial companies like Havas and Transpac. In these cases and others, they were not satisfied with an anonymous and soulless building. They root their buildings in their sites, as they did by retaining the riverside Coty factory building in Suresnes, or by turning the Hyatt Hotel in Ekaterinburg toward the *Cathedral-on-the-Blood*. Many architects write about method, but few who are not totally specialized in factory design have managed to create the kind of charter that Valode & Pistre imagined for Valéo. A proof of their modesty and their fundamental attachment to the real profession of architecture is the fact that other architects have been able to participate in the Valéo program, using the Valode & Pistre charter. A similar sense of coexistence with a client's needs and the presence of other architects is seen in the Renault Technocentre complex.

When architects reach out across the globe as Valode & Pistre are presently doing, a question that becomes more and more difficult to answer is just what ties them to their native country. In what sense are Valode & Pistre French architects? The answer to this question is fundamental to any understanding of their work. Their style is their method, and the method is deeply rooted in the most positive aspects of French culture. French was of course the global language of diplomacy until a recent date when English in its many forms swept forward. French remains a language capable of tremendous subtlety and variety. The elite graduates of France's *grandes écoles* cultivate an ability to analyze and solve problems that surely is related, as they say themselves, to the mathematical equilibriums of Descartes. The solution to a problem need not in itself appear to be French, but the method of analysis is, and the key to the solution is the method. The real success of Denis Valode and Jean Pistre has been their ability to adapt a way of thinking to an architectural strategy that works as well in Beijing as it does in Gouvieux. ∎

# L'Oréal Factory

| AULNAY-SOUS-BOIS - FRANCE |

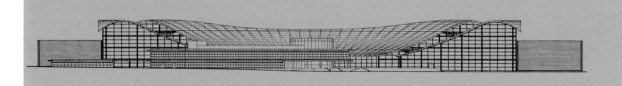

Completion date **1992**

Floor area **33,000 m²**

Client **L'Oréal**

Valode & Pistre participated in a competition organized by the cosmetics manufacturer for a factory that was intended from the first to be a strong element in the image of the firm. The program provided for clients of L'Oréal to be able to visit the facility, and more surprisingly, the company selected the factory to pioneer a new manufacturing method. In a bid to give workers more say in the process, it is organized around "mini assembly lines" that are roughly the size of a large kitchen. Intended not only for manufacturing but also for administrative offices and a research lab, the factory is shaped like a three-petaled flower, and has ample views onto a central garden. The architects' insistence on natural light in industrial facilities and horizontal views toward nature is evident in this design. One particularly outstanding feature of their design is the aluminum and polyethylene roof designed with the assistance of the engineer Peter Rice.

An aerial view of the L'Oréal factory facility shows the essential simplicity and logic of the plan. The central green space allows employees to look inward without feeling cut off from the world.

The petal-like
arrangement of the roof
of the building is in fact
indirectly inspired from
the shape of an orchid,
as the early sketches to
the left by Denis Valode
testify. The low curve
of the roof gives
a dynamic feeling
to the structure.

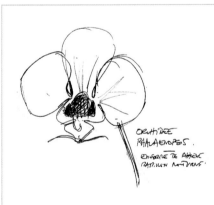

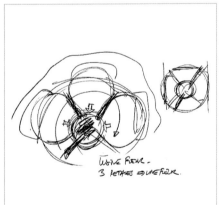

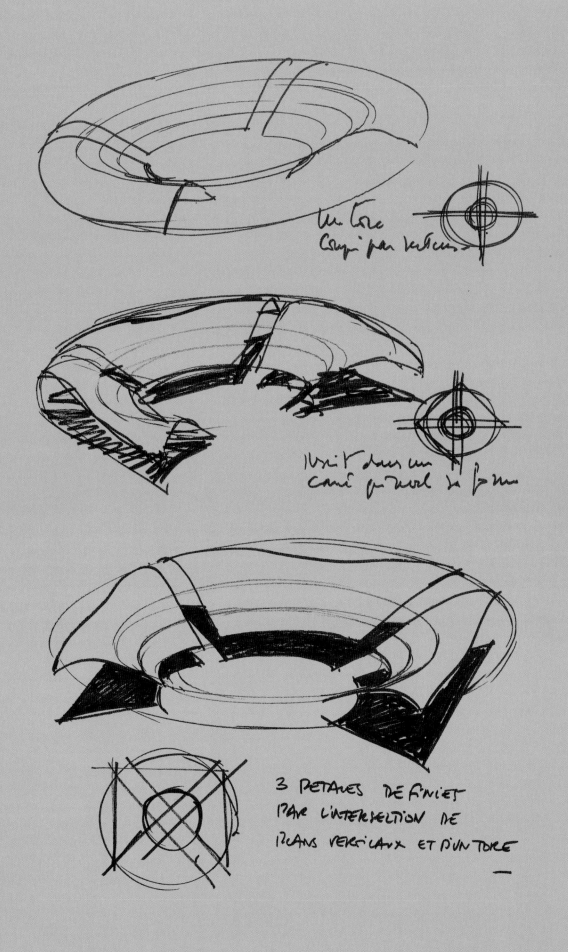

Un tore
coupé par verticaux

Inscrit dans un
carré qui veut sa forme

3 PÉTALES DÉFINIES
PAR L'INTERSECTION DE
PLANS VERTICAUX ET D'UN TORE

Denis Valode's sketches
use the word "petals"
to define the roof's
shape, and yet the final
design is stylized
to the point where
the original botanical
reference is almost
forgotten.
They also show that
a circle inscribed
in a square governs
the basic plan of
the building.

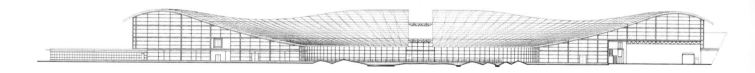

The arching lightness of the building is quite visible in the exterior image above, while the pictures and sketch to the right and on the next page demonstrate the architects' conviction that views toward the exterior are essential to the creation of a positive working atmosphere.

Rice, who created the firm RFR and who had worked with Renzo Piano on many projects including the Pompidou Center in Paris, was a key figure of the team here because the roof's complexity. The inverted pyramid joints he conceived sustain forces that come from as many as 14 different directions. Although computer assisted design had not reached its current levels of sophistication when this factory was conceived, computers and laser guided checking were used for the precision placement of 655 different types of panels in the curved roof. The advantage of this system was not only esthetic, but also practical, since it permitted the creation of manufacturing zones measuring 130 by 60 meters with no support columns. The torus form selected by the architects for the curving roof creates spaces that are varied and spatially more interesting than

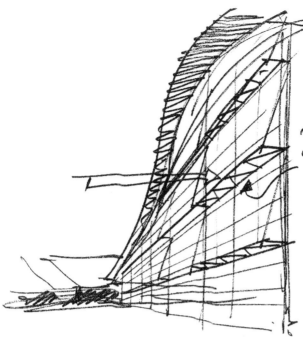

*repris de effort
de vent par des
portiques horizontals
triangulaires —*

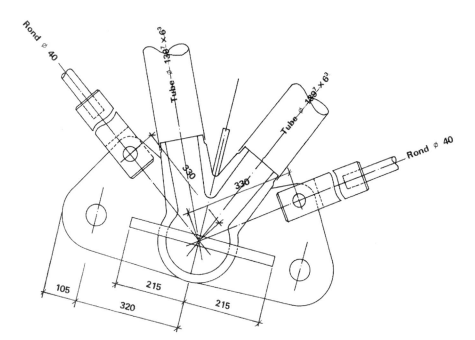

The complexity
and variety of the nodes
necessary to carry
the roof structure are
witness to the interest
of the architect's
in questions related
to engineering.
To the right, a space
frame and tie rods seem
to create a thicket
of structural elements,
but on the whole,
the design is extremely
light and airy.

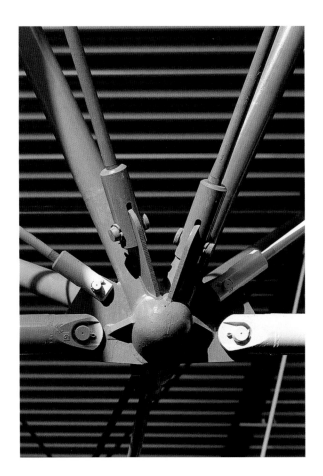

any flat roof could be. They have also managed to situate the manufacturing zones demanding greater ceiling height in the appropriate places.
Here as in other industrial facilities they have designed, where practical
requirements linked to manufacturing are complex, Valode & Pistre have
succeeded in imposing an esthetically pleasing solution that also meets
the needs of the client. The association of the flower shape with a perfume and cosmetics manufacturer might have been almost too obvious,
but in the hands of the architects, it becomes more of an abstraction than
a figurative reference in any sense. In this context, the spectacular roof
demonstrates that Valode & Pistre are less identifiable for any stylistic
characteristic than they are in terms of their approach. More simply put,
this roof does not look like anything else they have designed, but it fits
this situation perfectly and offers a truly new form to the client. They analyze each situation carefully and tend to propose innovative and unexpected solutions where form and function go hand in hand. Given the
prestige of the client and their avowed intention to make the Aulnay-sous-
Bois factory a showcase, this project established the relatively young
architects as a force to be reckoned with not only in France but internationally as well. ∎

The central garden plays a significant role in the design. Using prime space, that others might have filled with factory facilities, Valode & Pistre stick to their underlying idea that the factory should be a pleasant place, thus yielding higher productivity.

The garden and pond are relatively simple, like the curves of the roof, and indeed, there is a smooth flow from one to the other.

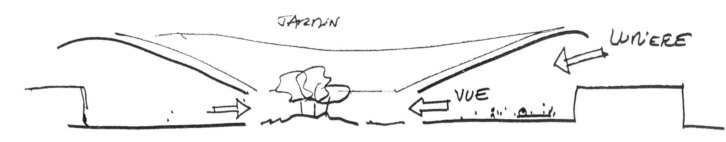

JARDIN          LUMIÈRE

VUE

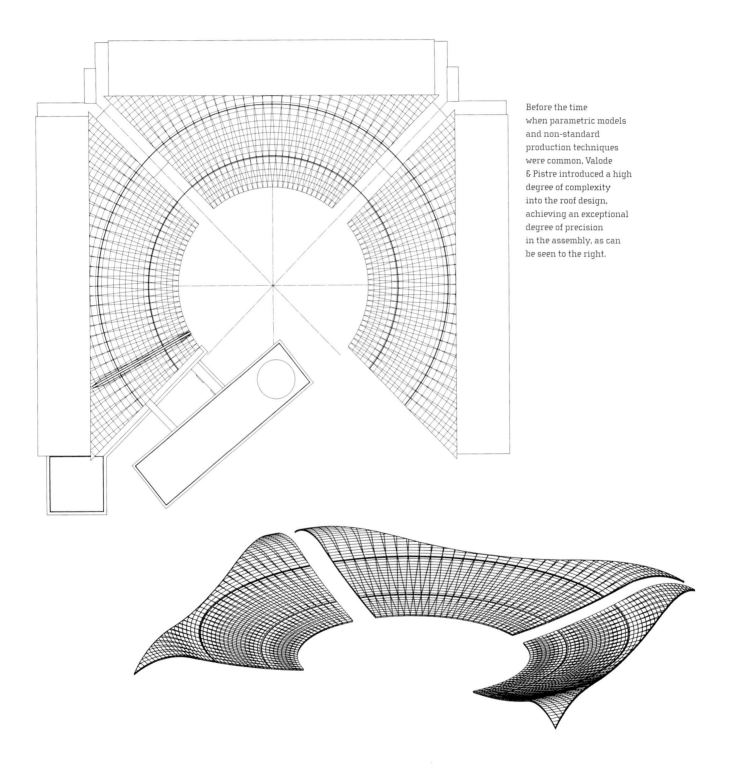

Before the time
when parametric models
and non-standard
production techniques
were common, Valode
& Pistre introduced a high
degree of complexity
into the roof design,
achieving an exceptional
degree of precision
in the assembly, as can
be seen to the right.

# UGC Bercy Ciné-Cité

| PARIS – FRANCE |

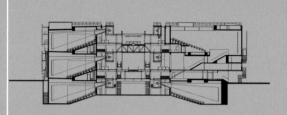

Completion date **1998**

Floor area **12,000 m²**

Program **Complex of 18 movie theaters and a cinema café**

Client **UGC**

Associated architect **A. Cattani - P. Chican**

# Strasbourg UGC Ciné-Cité

| STRASBOURG – FRANCE |

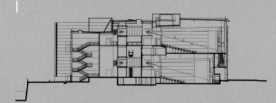

Completion date **1999**

Floor area **17,000 m²**

Program **Cinema complex comprising 21 movie theaters, 1 UGC « Max Cinema, » cinema café and restaurant**

Client **UGC**

When French movie theaters had mostly gone underground into claustrophobic spaces, Valode & Pistre dared to give the nobility of modern architecture back to the world of cinema.

The ample ceiling heights and spectacular openings of their UGC theaters give viewers the feeling that they are participating in an exceptional experience, and not in a run-of-the-mill commuter type of event.

■ The original plan for the Bercy Village project called for the Cour Saint-Emilion at its center, running perpendicularly to the Seine, to be closed off on the riverside by an office building. As it happens, Valode & Pistre were called on to design an entirely different kind of structure, and one that adds considerably to the attractivity of the complex. The UGC Ciné-Cité is an 18-movie theater complex whose design nods to the presence and alignment of the Bercy Village shopping area with its central glazed band in the alignment of the Cour Saint-Emilion. Since most Paris multiplex movie theaters are located in rather grim underground spaces, the Ciné-Cité was a real departure for the large UGC chain. The projection booths are visibly set outside of each theater, giving an immediate sense

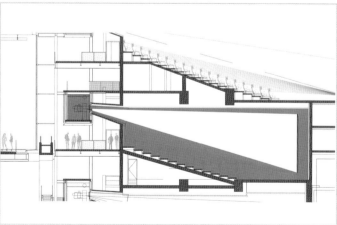

By hanging the projection booths outside of the theaters and allowing visitors to see them, the architects intend again to give back some of the excitement that going to the movies had lost with time and the "profit" driven style of architecture that had become so frequent. The idea is simple, but its application is another example of the architects' ability to give nobility to modern space.

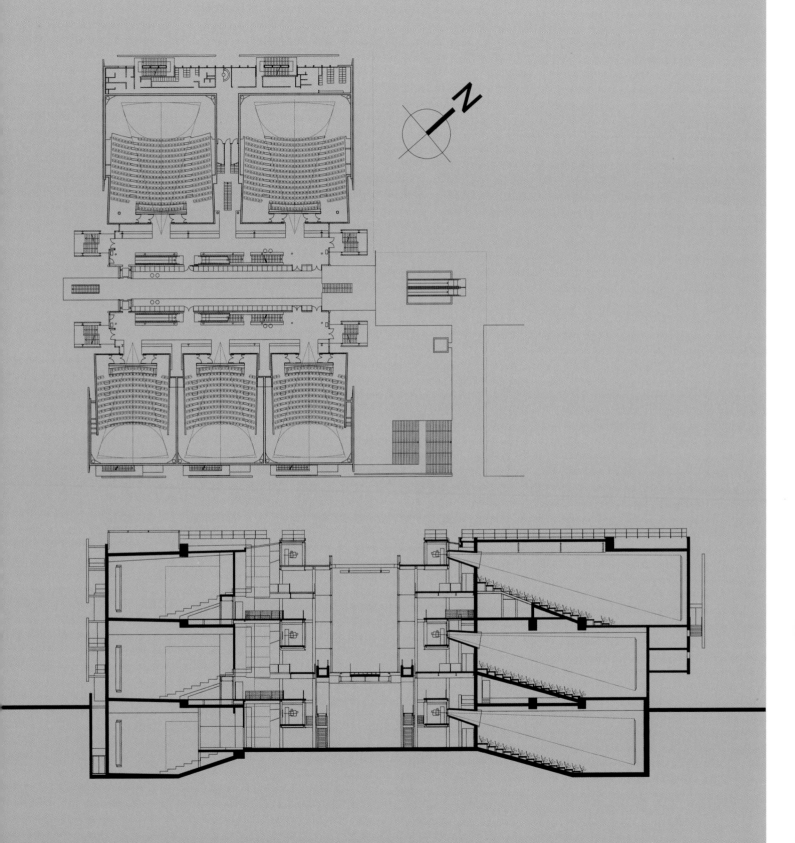

The plan below shows the Bercy Village structures as they lead directly to the movie theater. By virtue of the passageway driven through the building toward the river, the design is connected both with the city and with the immediate environment of the entrance area. Despite its obvious modernity, the theater ensemble is respectful of its urban environment.

of the activity within. Similarly, the actual movie screens are abstractly presented on the exterior façades as "luminescent panels of stainless steel mesh." Always attentive to the practical aspects of their projects, the architects designed the building so that entering and leaving movie-goers follow entirely separate paths. As the architects conclude their own description of this project, "Designed and built in association with Alberto Cattani and Pierre Chican, the UGC Bercy Ciné-Cité offers a journey beyond the real, through the looking glass, to join the make-believe world of the cinema."

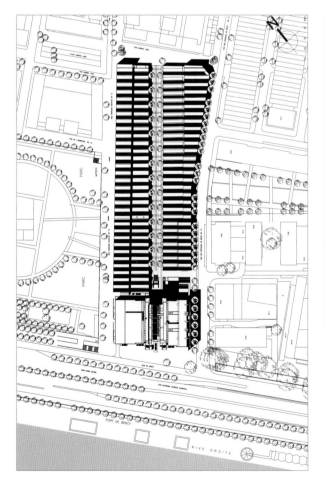

In obvious contrast to its industrial water-edge site, the theater complex stands out like an affirmation of the qualities of contemporary architecture, able, even here to attract crowds, and to do so in the context of the type of tight budget that the client appreciates.

The second UGC complex built by Valode & Pistre in Strasbourg is even larger than the first, with a total of 22 movie theaters. Located in an industrial zone near the Austerlitz port the structure presents a 120-meter façade along the RN4 roadway that leads to Germany. Made up of four blocks with superimposed theaters, separated by a double-height interior "street," the complex gives an impression of ample space, again not typical of most French movie architecture. Intended to stand out at night, the Strasbourg UGC Ciné-Cité animates a new area of the city that looked rather abandoned than animated until the arrival of Valode & Pistre.

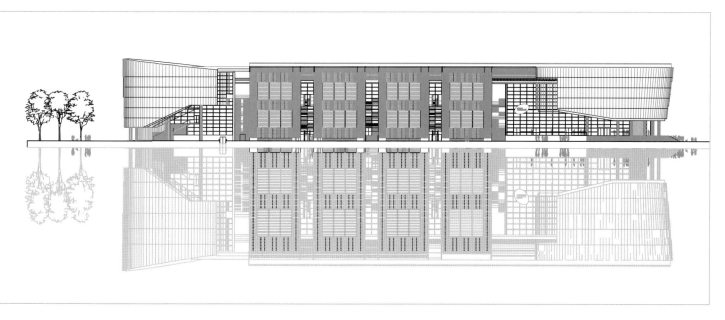

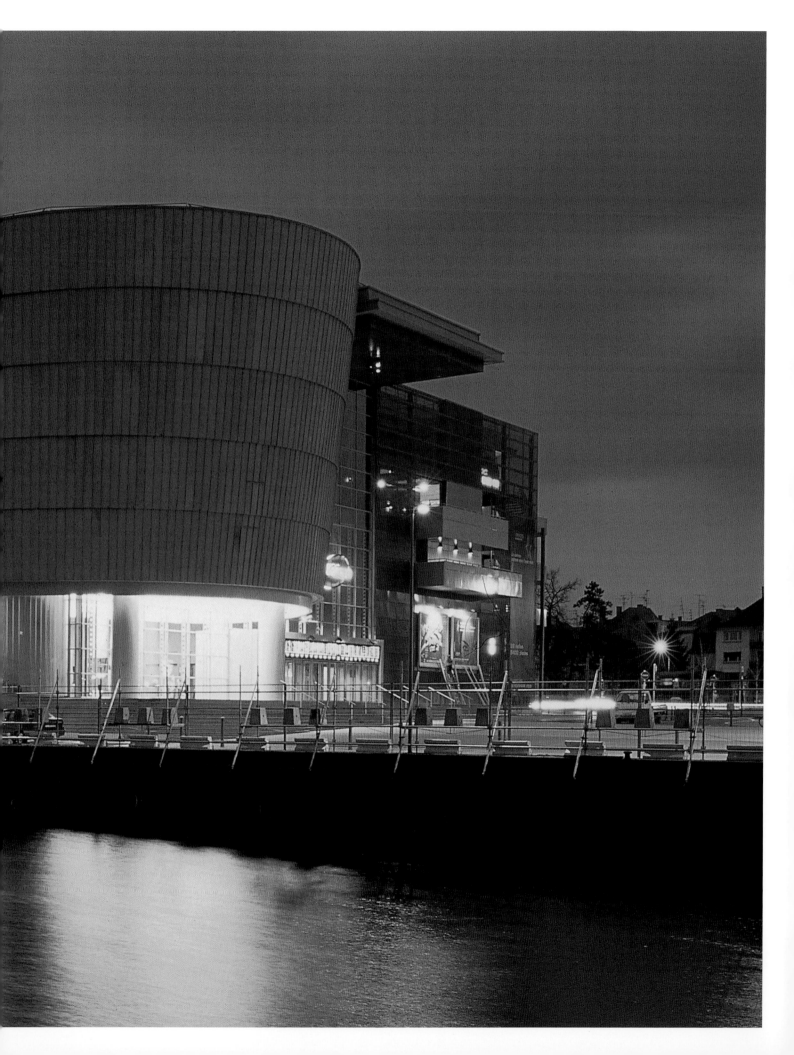

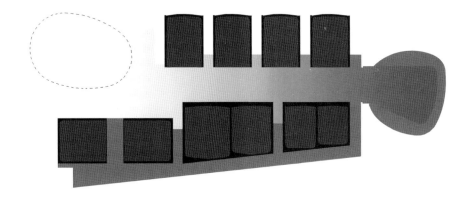

Both of these projects reveal the particular intelligence of the work of Valode & Pistre that allays an understanding of the mechanics of architecture itself, an interest in the function and use of their buildings, and an attention to both details and budgetary constraints. Simply put, there is a certain joy in designing that shows in their work, in particular when they are dealing with the general public as is certainly the case of the UGC projects. Valode & Pistre are also very comfortable with innovation in terms of redesigning building types from the ground up. Here, they listened to the client, but also imagined that their architecture was part of the spectacle that people come to pay and see. ■

A strong contrast between light and dark characterizes these evening views, as though the act of projection was also being acted out in the public spaces. The French call movie theaters *les salles obscures* (literally dark, or obscure rooms), but the magic of light is what makes this darkness not only tolerable but attractive.

# Paris Expo Hall 4
# Hall 5

| PARIS – FRANCE |

Completion date **1998**

Floor area **20,000 m²**

Client **Paris Expo**

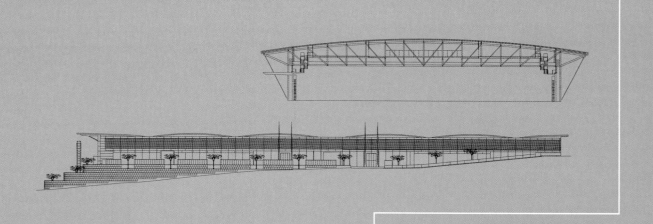

Completion date **2003**

Floor area **18,000 m²**

Client **Paris Expo**

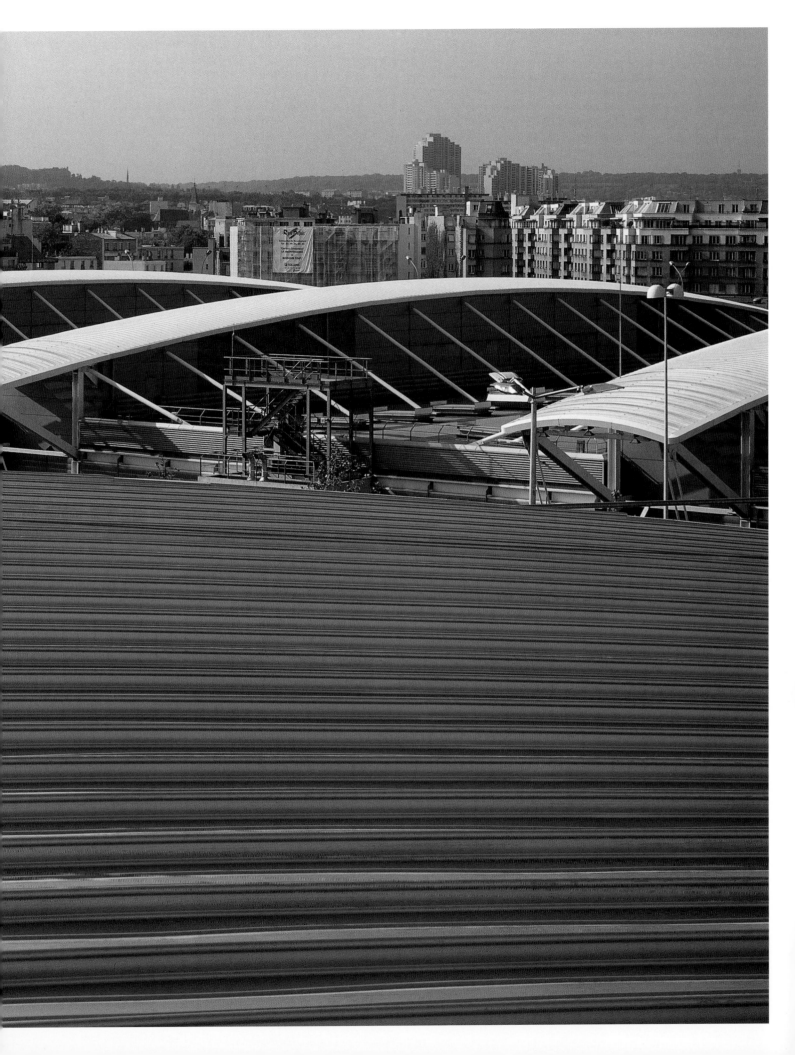

Valode & Pistre have
mastered the art
of creating very large
buildings that are
flexible enough for
exhibition organization
and yet fit into their
rather complicated
urban setting.

■ Valode & Pistre first became involved with the large convention center
and exhibition site at the Porte de Versailles in the west of Paris in 1991
when they participated in a competition organized by the city to renovate
the façade of the facility that faces the city. They responded that it was
useless to engage in a cosmetic action, but that the entire park should
be rebuilt over a ten-year period. Naturally, they lost the 1991 competition whose goal was more modest, but their ideas were to serve a purpose several years later. Created in 1925, the park included nine exhibition pavilions, the last of which had been built in the 1970's. Crossed by
the ring road of Paris, the site was ill adapted to modern exhibitions, with
difficult truck access. In 1996, the president of the facilities consulted
several architects, including Norman Foster before choosing Valode &
Pistre to engage in precisely the kind of major renovation they had

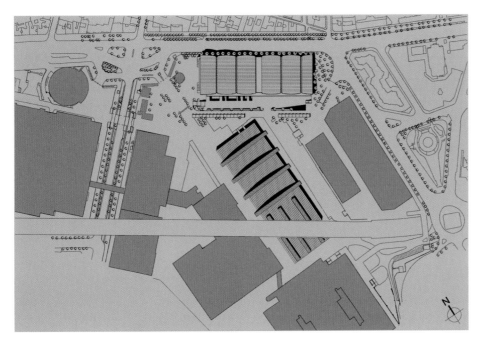

Despite their bulk, the Paris Expo facilities appear to make a bow to the more domestic scale of the Paris streets just opposite.

Crossed by the busy
circular boulevard,
the Paris Expo site
is as intensely urban
as any in the French
capital. The architects
have borrowed from
the vocabulary of
industrial architecture,
as well they might given
the size of these
structures. Making use
of their own passion
for engineering,
they have offered high,
column free space
on a scale almost
unheard of in Paris.

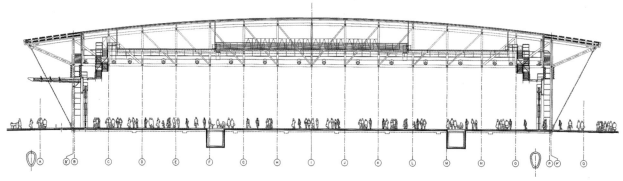

A view above the roofs
of the Valode & Pistre
building reveals the
apartment buildings
opposite, many of them
still in a style formed
at the time of the work
on Paris carried out
by the Baron Georges
Haussmann (1809-1892)
beginning in the 1860's.

The profile of their new
building (right) echoes
the stone bases of the
older structures, but
becomes progressively
lighter as it rises.

proposed five years earlier. With a total built area of about 200,000 m², the park already exceeded the allowable quota, but city officials agreed to the renovation on the condition that the final floor area remain unchanged. The first structure to be completed was Hall 4, a multi-purpose facility 250 meters long, by 84 meters wide with a clear interior height of 10.5 meters. With beams spanning the full 84-meter width, technical ducts in the ceilings and further technical spaces below grade, Hall 4 offers an exceptional size and flexibility. Linear skylights accompany the spanning beams, laid out in an east-west arrangement. The second completed facility was Hall 5, with its 200-meter long façade engaging the residential scale of the Boulevard Lefebvre. Large aluminum panels divided by curtain wall glazing sit atop a concrete base, colored to resemble the limestone façades of the apartment buildings opposite. Because of a natural slope in the site, the architects decided to superimpose two exhibition spaces, one on top of the other. Suspended ceilings and floors containing the technical conduits serve 70-meter wide column free

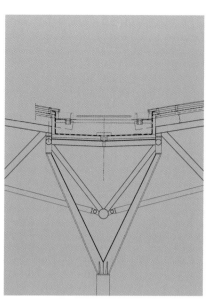

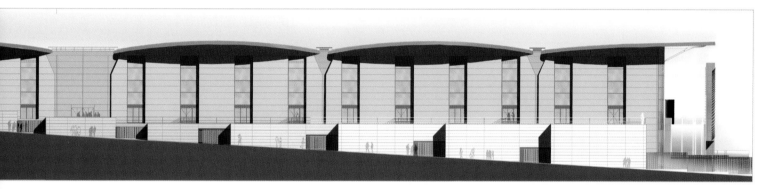

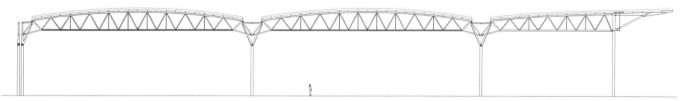

The very light columns
and arching spans
of the exhibition spaces
may recall typical
industrial sheds, on
the scale of those erected
for the railway stations
of Paris in the 19th
century, but here, both
the materials and the
technical characteristics
of the design bring an
entirely new approach
to exhibition space.

The architects
apparently enjoy
a strong contrast
between transparency
and opacity, with large
hovering volumes (right)
giving way to enormous
openings toward
the city and the sky.
Here, as elsewhere
in their work, efficiency
is the goal, with the
decided intention
to make the visitor
feel at ease.

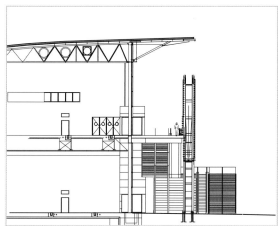

spaces. A 65-meter roof overhang and curved canopies render the entrance to Hall 5 both visible and visually exciting, while an esplanade slightly larger than one hectare connects the new building to the rest of the park. Working with a client described by Denis Valode as having a "realistic idea of costs and a strict budget," the architects succeeded in renewing a building type that does not often benefit from "quality" design. Given their preoccupation with matters of cost, exhibition facilities often opt for simple "shed" type designs that do the exhibitors little justice. Valode & Pistre, with their typical enthusiasm have taken ongoing project in hand and shown that with the same budgets, it is possible to create attractive, practical and technically advanced buildings. Their next addition to the park is called Hall 7, and it will form the heart of the facility, whose continuous activity has ruled out any possibility of beeing closed down entirely while construction goes on. ∎

# Valéo Generic
# Factory

| VESZPREM – HUNGARY |
Completion date **2000**
Floor area **11,000 m²**
Program **Electric Systems Factory**

| SAN LUIS POTOSI – MEXICO |
Completion date **2001**
Floor area **10,000 m²**
Program **Electric Systems Factory**

| SKAWINA – POLAND |
**Phase 1** Completion date **2001**
Floor area **20,000 m²**
Program **Engine Cooling Factory**
**Phase 2** Completion date **2003**
Floor area **10,000 m²**
Program **Wipers System Factory**

| BOUZNIKA – MOROCCO |
Completion date **2002**
Floor area **21,000 m²**
Program **Connective Systems Factory**

| ZEBRAK – CZECH REPUBLIC |
Completion date **2003**
Floor area **16,000 m²**
Program **Climate Control Factory**

| CHRZANOW – POLAND |
**Phase 1** Completion date **2002**
Floor area **23,000 m²**
**Phase 2** Completion date **2005**
Floor area **28,000 m²**
Program **Lighting Systems Factory**

Despite being a general scheme, not necessarily intended for any one location, the Valéo plants are differentiated through the presence of a locally-created art work, and landscaping that makes them fit into their specific sites. Ample ceiling heights, natural light and views to the exterior are some of the hallmarks of the factories.

■ The Valéo Generic Factory is one of the most unusual and interesting of the projects of Valode & Pistre. Valéo is a multi-national automobile equipment maker, and the architects have set out to conceive a company charter for the construction of factories as opposed to single facilities. As they say, "The Generic Factory refers to no particular project but is a design guide, incorporating the Valéo design criteria that can be adapted to any particular situation, facilitating the elaboration of any given project." The point is that Valode & Pistre are not necessarily the only architects to work on these projects – rather they have attempted to set the rules that other, local architects might follow. One priority of the architects has been to charter a hierarchy for the various industrial spaces required by any factory. The production space is conceived as a "movie set" with facilities such as administrative offices and restaurants grouped off to one side.

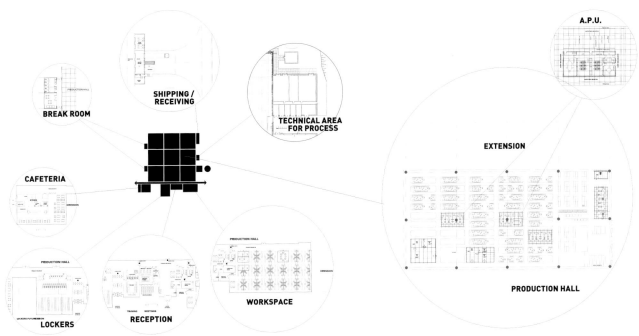

BREAK ROOM

SHIPPING /
RECEIVING

TECHNICAL AREA
FOR PROCESS

A.P.U.

EXTENSION

CAFETERIA

LOCKERS

RECEPTION

WORKSPACE

PRODUCTION HALL

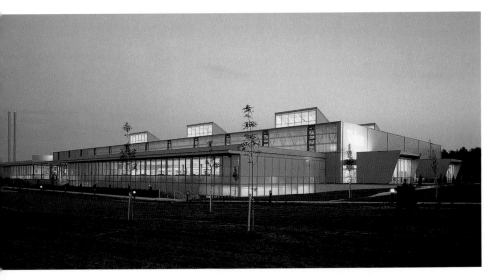

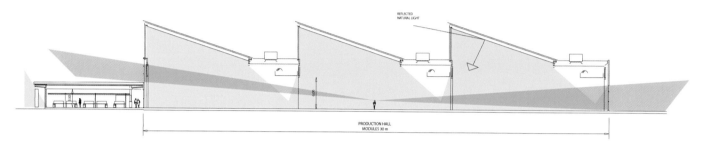

REFLECTED
NATURAL LIGHT

PRODUCTION HALL
MODULES 30 m

Roof schemes can
be altered according
to the precise type of
manufacturing being
done, but they all bring
daylight onto the factory
floor. Services are
concentrated in
a modular arrangement
on one side of the
factories as indicated
in the plans to the right,
and a strict grid system
is applied throughout.

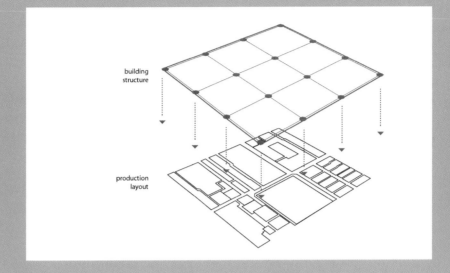

building
structure

production
layout

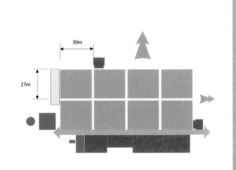

30m

27m

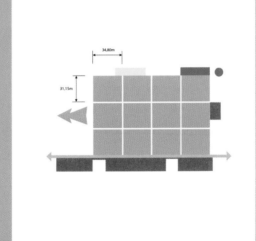

34,80m

31,15m

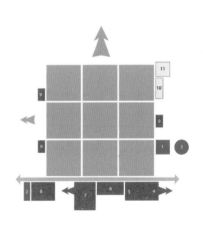

11

10

9

9

9

1

3

2 8

7

6 5 4

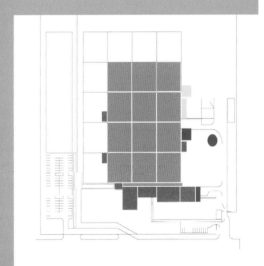

Although the Valéo factories are not as unique as the L'Oréal facility featured in this volume, they retain something of the open, airy spirit of the architects' earlier foray into the purely industrial realm.

Major axes are selected for the factory and left freely accessible under all circumstances. Trucks must arrive at the factories without ever crossing the path of pedestrians. Future enlargements are always provided for on the basis of a firmly imposed grid, usually 30-meter squares. The architects insist on the need for natural light within the factory, frequent views to the exterior and an ample ceiling height. The nature of the roof of each factory varies according to the density of its technological requirements, with more sophisticated production demanding more roof installations than simple manufacturing tasks. Valéo uses a system of moveable inspection units that can be placed anywhere in the factories to examine production quality. This too is provided for in the generic design. As Jean Pistre says, "We respect the production process, but that is not the basis of our thinking. Some factors like the separation of vehicular and pedestrian traffic are just not negotiable in our opinion. We feel that even complex production processes do not necessarily impose a specific geometry

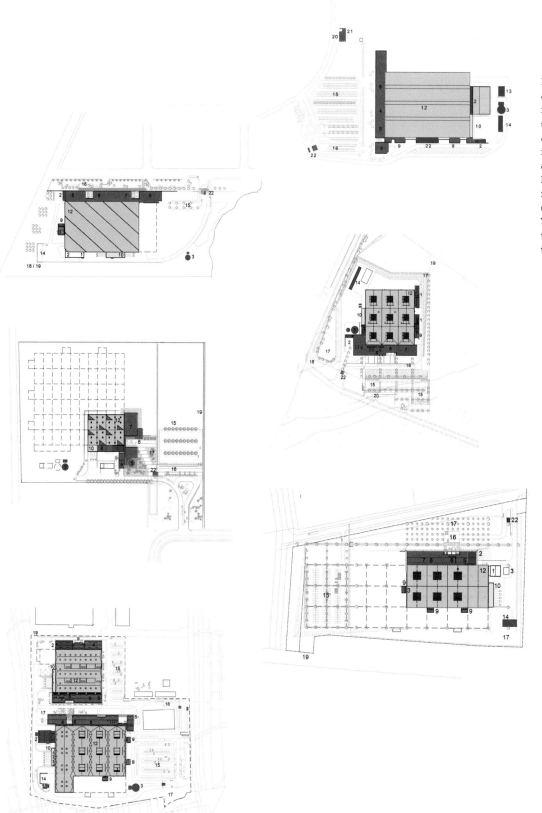

Looking something like a board game, the plans for the Valéo factories succeed in taking into account the numerous manufacturing arrangements required by the client while in fact improving the efficiency of the process. To the right, skylights take an ample place in the roofs of the plants.

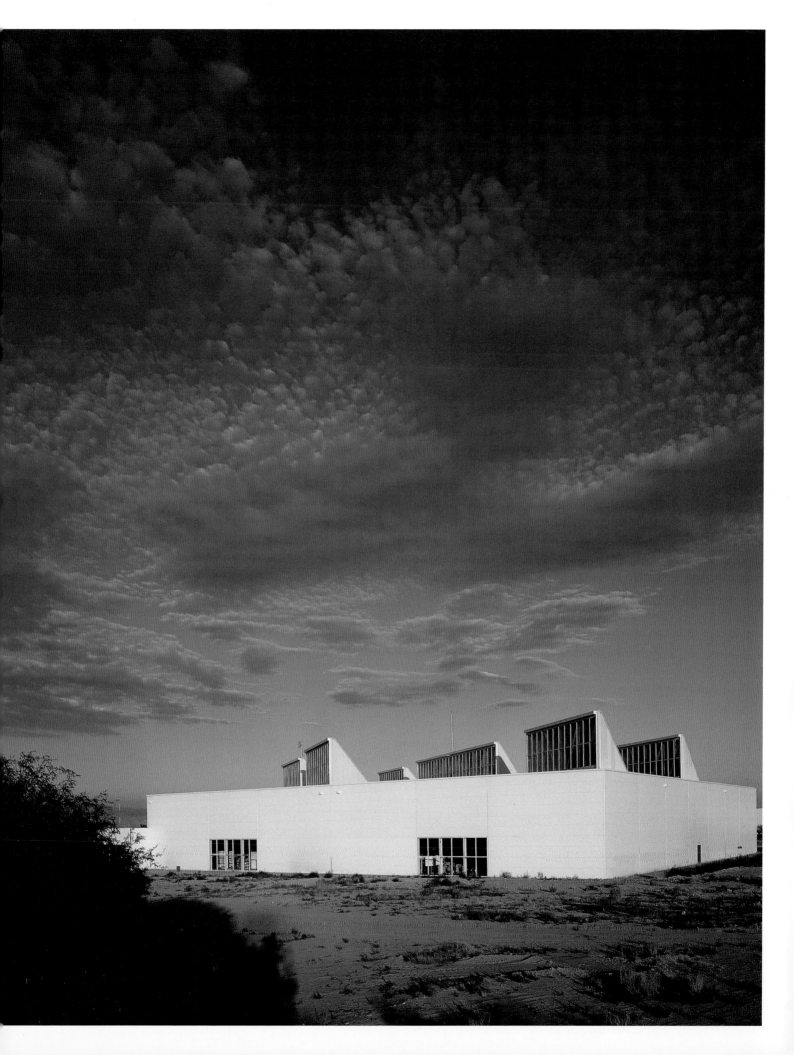

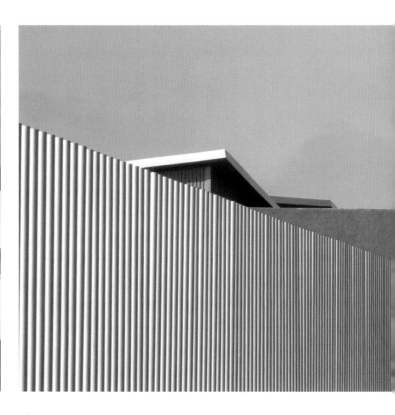

on a factory. Almost everything can be done differently, and discovering new ways of doing things, is what we are fascinated by." Valéo is particularly well suited to an open "democratic" type of factory, because the firm makes no distinction between office and factory personnel, both in terms of prestige and of salary. Another particularity of the firm is their insistence that factories can be demolished after ten years without adverse effects on the environment. "In the context of globalization," says Jean Pistre, "we feel that it is all the more important to be clear and simple. People have to understand almost instinctively why the factory is designed the way it is." The architects have participated in the selection of local artists to work in each factory, giving importance to each location even while creating a global design. When asked if his own rather idealistic description of the ambitions of the architects don't revert to the early modern logic that architecture could improve the life of people, an unapologetic Jean Pistre answers, "I ask myself if improving peoples' lives isn't the most important task of architecture." ∎

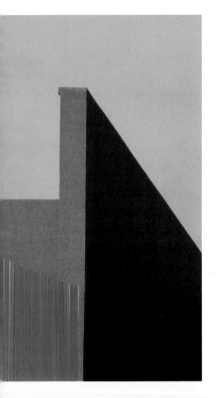

Although the goal of the architects was not necessarily to break new ground on the esthetic front, it is interesting to note that their pursuit of manufacturing efficiency has in fact created very attractive buildings that are pleasant to use for their staff. Overall, by increasing worker and thus consumer satisfaction, the architects have shown that good design pays back any reasonable investment.

# Bercy Village

| PARIS - FRANCE |

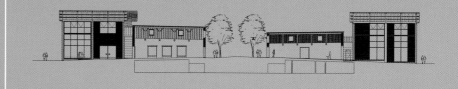

Completion date **2001**

Floor area **30,000 m²**

Client **Altarea**

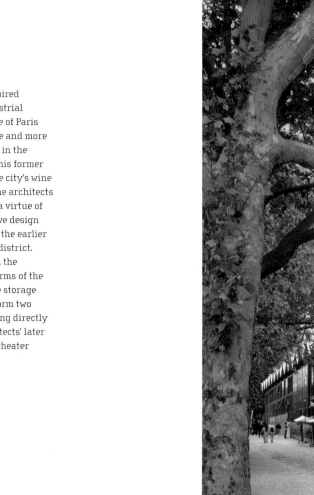

Clearly inspired by the industrial architecture of Paris on the whole and more specifically in the context of this former center of the city's wine business, the architects have made a virtue of the repetitive design imposed by the earlier warehouse district. To the right, the extended forms of the former wine storage buildings form two bands leading directly to the architects' later UGC movie theater complex.

■ As part of a large urban renewal plan for the east of Paris, the city organized a competition in 1990 for the reuse of a series of wine warehouses. Set in parallel bands running perpendicularly towards the Seine, these late 19ᵗʰ century structures were in poor condition for the most part. As winners of the competition, Valode & Pistre proposed an innovative solution: "We wanted to create a continuity with the existing architecture, to make something contemporary with what existed," says Denis Valode. "We reconstituted some of the warehouses, and behind them, we designed higher buildings. The basic pattern runs perpendicularly to the river, but there are also passageways parallel to the Seine. There is a difference of scale that decreases as one approaches through the parallel entries and finally reaches the central street. Our competitors proposed to cover this alley, but we left it open like a real old Parisian street with paving stones and the original rails that allowed large wine barrels to be moved." A "folded" or zigzag zinc roof characterizes the new buildings and constitutes the symbol of the new shopping district. "We have made a consistent effort to make it apparent the difference between old and new

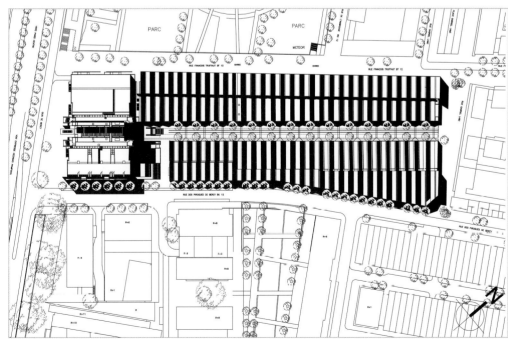

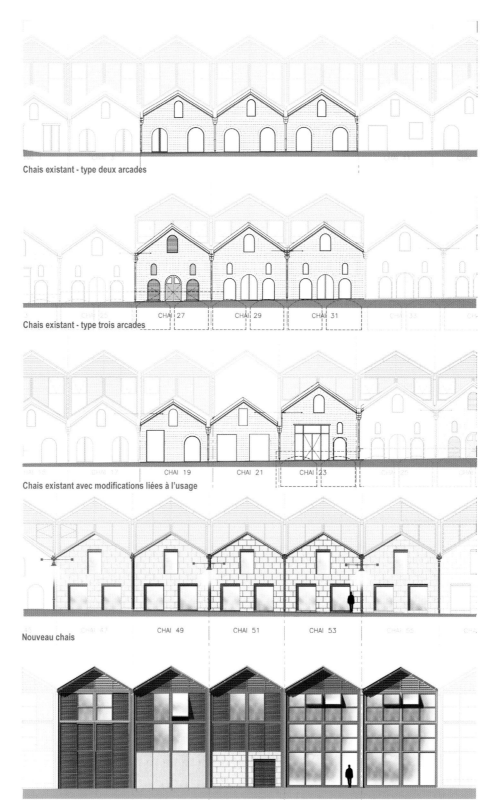

Chais existant - type deux arcades

Chais existant - type trois arcades

Chais existant avec modifications liées à l'usage

Nouveau chais

Bâtiment plissé

Making elegant use of the variety of existing buildings, either by simply renovating them, restoring them entirely, or going on to create modern façades in a similar spirit, Valode & Pistre have breathed new life into Bercy. By calling on the old buildings as they stood in some cases, they preserve the cachet that would have been lost had a new, air-conditioned mall been built in their place.

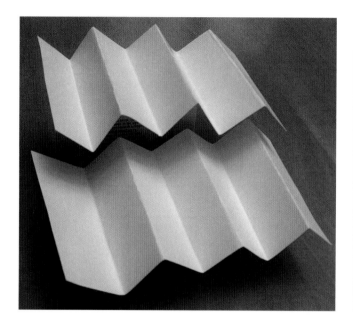

The repetitive folded-structure of the roofs is visible both in the photograph below and in the actual folded pieces of paper to the left. Despite an almost mass-produced plan, Bercy Village has a distinctly Parisian flavor, born of its remaining old stones, including the cobblestones of the streets, seen to the right during a typically crowded shopping day and on the next page.

in our restoration of the existing buildings. We referred to the old covered markets of Paris when we designed the folded roof pattern of the new buildings – in other words, even the contemporary parts of the project refer back to the old cast iron market structures," says Valode. Bercy Village is part of a larger commercial and residential complex including a new park, where Valode & Pistre have also designed a large UGC movie theater. The 14-hectare Bercy Park was completed in 1995 as part of a plan to give some life to almost abandoned areas near the new French Ministry of Finance and the *Palais Omnisport* indoor arena along the right bank of the Seine. Although the actual Bercy Village area is run by a single firm that assures the respect for the original design by Valode & Pistre, some clients, such as Club Med called on other architects who did not necessarily adhere to the spirit conceived by the French team. The Bercy 2

Glass, wood and metal replace the stone of the old Bercy in the newer structures, but their rhythm and scale are obviously inspired by the architecture of the wine district.

Pedestrians are given priority here, as is rarely the case in the French capital, adding to the appeal of the project.

shopping mall is nearby (Renzo Piano and Jean-François Blassel, 1990), as is Frank Gehry's former American Center (1994). Valode & Pistre worked with the urban development coordinator for Bercy, the architect Michel Macary. The fact that the architects retained the atmosphere of the wine warehouses is surely a major reason for the outstanding success of their project, which draws thousands of visitors to shops and restaurants every weekend. The underlying idea of this project has to do with the very building type of shopping centers. "Traditionally," says Denis Valode, "shopping centers were places of what I would call 'non-architecture,' completely covered and sealed off from their environments, somewhere at the periphery of a large city. That was a pity – a shopping area should be at the origin of the life of an urban area. Rather than allowing architecture to be absent from shopping centers, we think it should be seen as the real source of neighborhood gathering and activity." ∎

# Cap Gemini /
# Ernst & Young University

| GOUVIEUX – FRANCE |

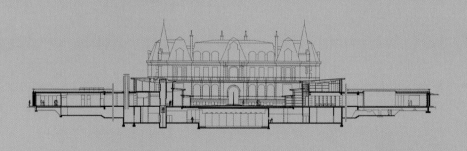

Completion date **2002**

Floor area **23,000 m²**

Client **Cap Gemini / Ernst & Young**

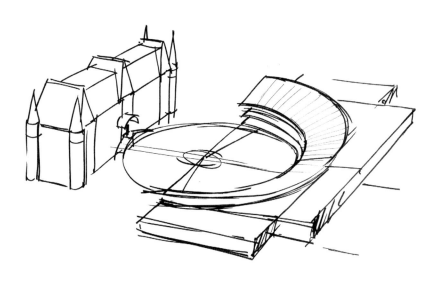

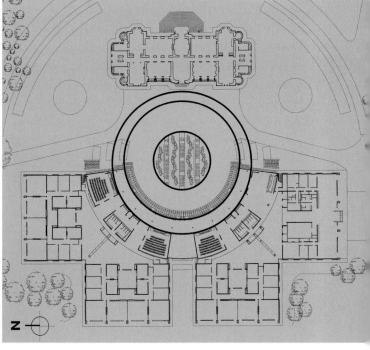

A sketch by Denis Valode above left, and the plan to the left show how the architects resolved the problem posed by the existing chateau. Both the garden and the new architecture appear to have been generated by the older rectangle, gathering in front of the former Rothschild residence as though French tradition were the source of the client's corporate culture.

■ A thoroughly modern company, Cap Gemini / Ernst & Young, has some 90,000 employees spread all over the world. Despite the firm's well-established reputation for quality service, its directors felt the need to create a center where personnel could meet for carefully organized seminars. Naturally, the architecture of this university was an important element in affirming the discreet solidity and permanence of the company as the very choice of the site indicates. Set in Gouvieux near the residence and offices of the Aga Khan (Aiglemont) and close to the Chateau of Chantilly, the 50-hectare property was cleared by monks before becoming a "pleasure garden" under Louis XV. Purchased by the Rothschild family in the late 19th century, the park saw the construction of a chateau in what Denis Valode describes as "Disney style," a sort of assemblage of historic references. Significantly, in a country used to listing almost any castle, this Rothschild house was never listed and therefore not subjected to any particular official protection. Used as a headquarters for the German air force during World War II, the building was converted into a library by the Jesuits after the War. Denis Valode explains that for Cap Gemini / Ernst & Young,

Sweeping curves and modern materials contrast with the chateau, seen just opposite in the photo on the left and in the sketch. In this way, it is clear that the client seeks to build on an ancient tradition, while maintaining extreme modernity. Valode & Pistre thus succeed in transmitting a bit of corporate philosophy while solving the architectural issues in an elegant manner.

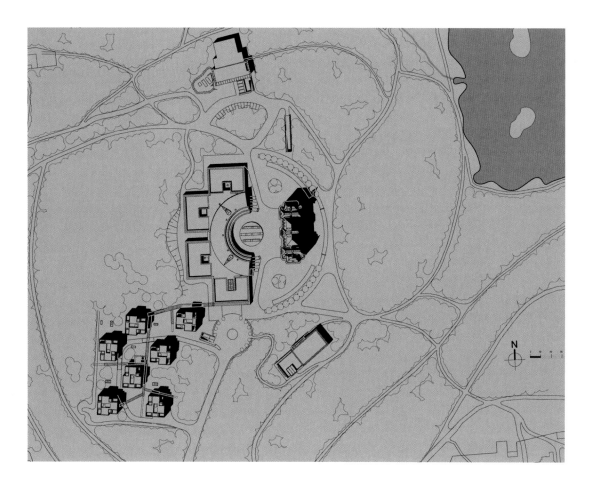

The curved and stepped design of the semicircular pavilion facing the chateau allows its bulk to avoid overwhelming the older building just opposite. The elevations below show that the chateau remains twice as high as the new buildings. A site plan to the left shows the other buildings dispersed in the parkland near the site's heart.

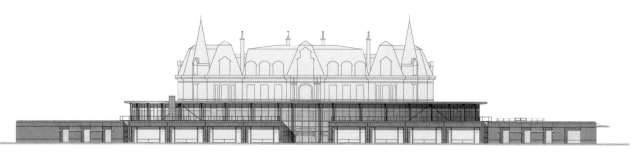

as an international firm with a French base, it was of interest to highlight their own attachment to continuity in business relations by using the chateau as a quintessential symbol. The problem for the architects was how to deal with this historic pile and still project an image of modernity. They looked to the work of Edwin Lutyens for inspiration, and decided that a low, semi-circular building set opposite the chateau, would provide the needed contrast while not rejecting harmony with the past. Like most French gardens, the design here calls on a strong axial composition whose point of origin is the center of the chateau. The implication of this gesture is that a very modern firm can nonetheless look to its roots and to a continuity with the past. Demolishing an undistinguished addition to the chateau that had been made by the Jesuits, Valode & Pistre went so far as to create a meticulous copy of one wing of the chateau that had not

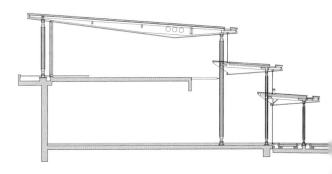

An elegant and simple design for the steel columns appears to make light of the weight that they actually carry. Combining wood and metal the architects play on the contrast of heaviness and lightness, sometimes making the visitor wonder just how the structure holds up.

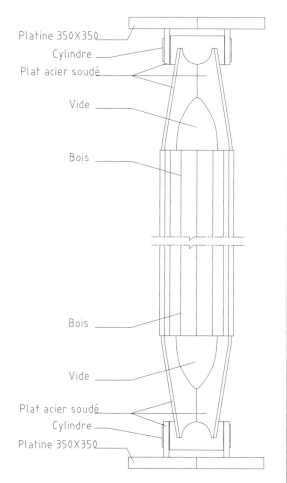

Platine 350X350
Cylindre
Plat acier soudé
Vide
Bois
Bois
Vide
Plat acier soudé
Cylindre
Platine 350X350

The section to the right
shows that much
of the volume of the new
structure (such as the
auditorium) is actually
hidden below grade
under the garden
that separates the
chateau from the work
of Valode & Pistre.

The rather strict lines
seen in the interior
image to the right
actually blend in quite
well with another French
tradition, that of
gardens originated
or mastered by
André Le Nôtre.

survived the 20th century. The careful recreation of old buildings, in this case a veritable imitation of the existing design, has not been to the taste of many architects since the Post-Modern days, but it seems quite natural for Valode & Pistre. Despite a very detailed program submitted to the architects who participated in the competition for this facility won by Valode & Pistre, they were left free to demolish the original chateau, had they wished to do so. Here, as elsewhere, the architects have shown a pronounced willingness to deal with the vestiges of the past even as they build very modern buildings. Particularly in France's rich historic environment this openness to the past is a strong point for the architects, as is their interest, expressed here too, in landscape design. Lodgings and leisure facilities, in a decidedly modern style dot the rest of the park at a slight remove from the central complex. ∎

# PB12 Office Tower

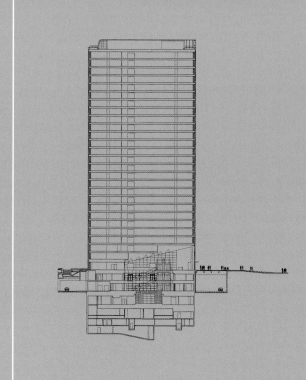

Completion date **2002**

Floor area **36,000 m²**

Client **Axa / Cogedim**

Interior architect **Germanaz**

It seems that Valode & Pistre are often given the task of making old architecture modern. In the case of the PB 12 project, the original building, the 1970 Tour Crédit Lyonnais, located on the southern side of La Défense, has become all but invisible after their intervention. The owner of the building, the insurance company AXA, determined that demolition of the old structure would be prohibitively expensive, and after a competition in which Arquitectonica from Miami participated, Valode & Pistre suggested a radical reconstruction, adding approximately 200 m² per floor, they effectively did away with the original load-bearing façade. Increasing the average floor area from 800 m² to 1,000 m² and updating the technical facilities of the tower, the architects were able to offer spaces considered almost ideal in their configuration for potential occupants. With pillars every 1.4 meters, the Crédit Lyonnais tower had been

Like aging nuclear reactors, old office towers are more of a problem than they seem. They are very expensive to demolish. At the request of the client, did a masterful job in bringing the former Crédit Lyonnais building into the 21ˢᵗ century.

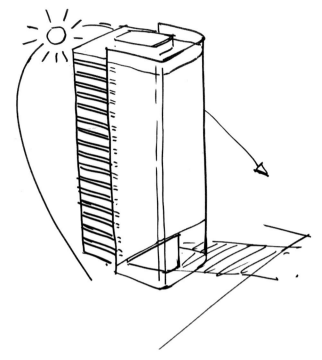

The shimmering exterior cladding was inspired by the "opalescent sheen of an oyster shell," as Denis Valude says. Cladding design was carefully studied to avoid excessive solar gain.

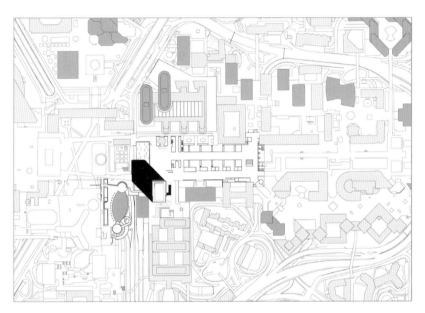

A sketch by Valode (right) shows how the plan for the Opus 12 allows light into the previously underused levels located below grade. Reflecting its neighbors, the structure seen to the left takes on a subtlety and a modern smoothness that most other buildings in the area lack.

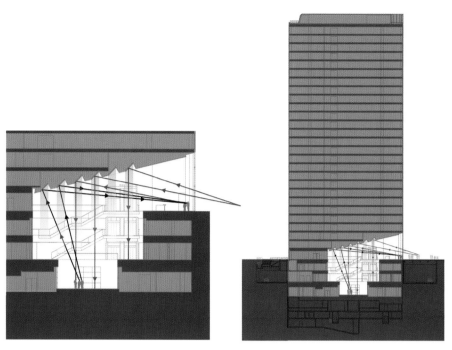

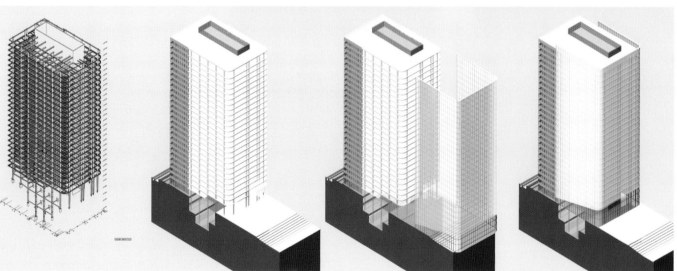

Drawings show the progressive refitting of the old building. At the top of the page, the architects' careful study of the lighting conditions of the below-grade atrium was calculated to add value to these hitherto neglected spaces.

practically opaque, rendering any real modernization extremely difficult. Essentially identical on each side, the old building was reworked in the direction of the Esplanade of La Défense by the architects, and in the process, the new façade was freed from the load-bearing. Since local building regulations required that the floor area of the building not be increased by the work, the architects sought to make use of the relatively large, but totally enclosed underground space of the first structure. They dug a hole, creating a courtyard that brings light into a cafeteria and the meeting rooms that are located below grade, and offering daylight to visitors emerging from the underground parking lot. The floor area deducted by the creation of this opening could then be added in the 27 floors above the Esplanade. The open space below grade has also permitted the architects to create what is essentially a new and bright entrance to a building that had previously been almost devoid of a recognizable front or back.

Drawings of the building
show the space added
by the reconstruction
efforts. Stairways and
transparent elevator
shafts give the kind
of modern aspect often
seen in the work
of Valode & Pistre.

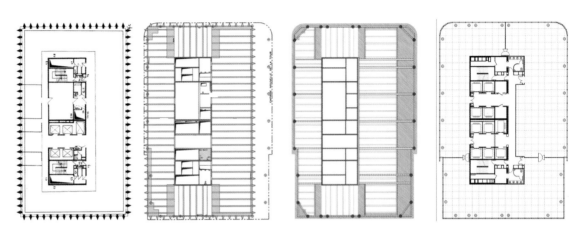

The building now offers views toward the Arch de la Défense, a luxury that the old structure did only in a more limited way. Lightness and a typical contrast between opacity and transparency are the hallmarks of the entrance area of the building.

Technically very challenging the approach of Valode & Pistre involved building a new superstructure outside the walls of the existing building, driving beams into the core of the building to create a new support system, and then demolishing the old load-bearing façade from the top down, floor by floor. The new façade was then put in place from the top up, giving what Denis Valode calls "an opalescent sheen like the inside of an oyster shell to the exterior – almost like a precious jewel." The semi-reflective glass used here offers a significant sun shield, improving the energy performance of the tower. The job also involved reinforcing the existing core to compensate the greater wind stress on a larger façade, but in this as in other matters, the architects called on the knowledge of the engineer who had worked on the building in 1970. The early development of La Défense and other modern areas of Paris like the Front de Seine in the 15th arrondissement, where Valode & Pistre are also working, was characterized by curious and complicated architectural forms that have aged poorly. Especially in the case of a tower where demolition costs are high, the PB12 project, completed for approximately 10 to 15% more than it would have cost to erect a new building on an empty piece of land, is an exemplary case of urban reuse. ∎

# Transpac Office Building

| PARIS - FRANCE |

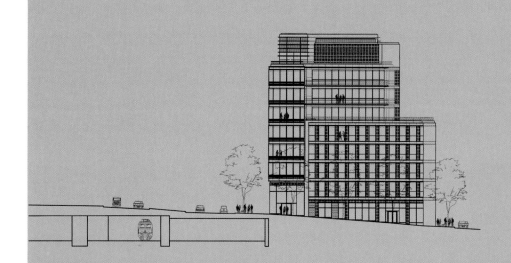

Completion date **2002**

Floor area **19,000 m²**

Program **Offices, restaurant, retail space**

Client **Meunier Promotion**

Taking on a ship-like form, with its prow to the left of the image above, the Transpac building belies its bulk through a layered smoothness, with an insistent horizontal banding that gives an impression of movement.

■ France has a long history of purpose designed cities and neighborhoods – the so-called Villes Nouvelles and "mini-Manhattans" like the Front de Seine and La Défense areas of Paris. Very often, these urban development zones, or entirely new constructions as in the case of the Villes Nouvelles, are carefully thought out, on paper. The reality is much less advantageous, as the PB12 and Beaugrenelle projects of Valode & Pistre have shown. They have successfully intervened to give a sense of true modernity to buildings that were originally heavy-handed and inefficient. Part of the difficulty in the French system may be the priority given to engineers, graduates of the famous Ponts et Chaussées school who have always been determined to show their prowess, often at the expense of architecture. Some of these lessons appear to have been learned with the newest development area in Paris, in the 13th arrondissement, the Seine Rive Gauche district near Dominique Perrault's National Library. Working on the basis of a master plan conceived by the Pritzker Prize

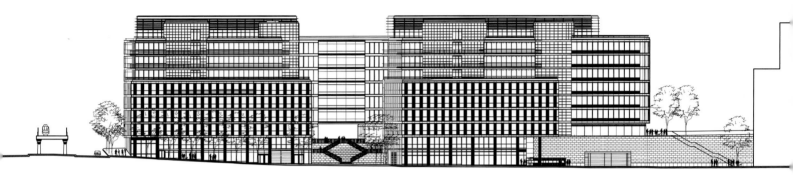

A site plan and
an elevation show how
the architects have dealt
with the awkward,
triangular site,
essentially cutting
the building in two and
allowing a passageway
to penetrate the
structure in the middle.
The gentle curve of
the avenue is assumed
by the part of the
building to the right
in the site plan.

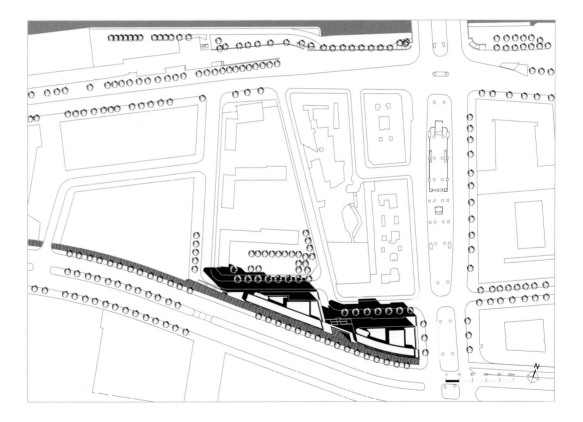

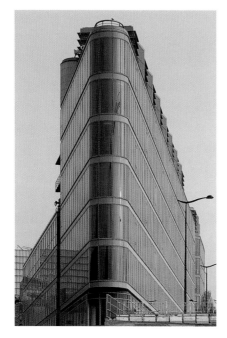
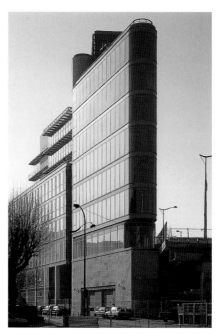

Near an old elevated line of the Paris subway, the Transpac building shows its layered composition in the image below. Above, and in the sketch to the right, the rounded prow of the structure diminishes its apparent mass and recalls that the Seine is close by.

The detailing of the building, apparent in the image to the left of the prow is both accomplished and visually arresting. Sections and a plan (below) show the layering of the structure, including its levels below grade. The actual shapes of the buildings seen in the plan are more irregular than photographs usually reveal.

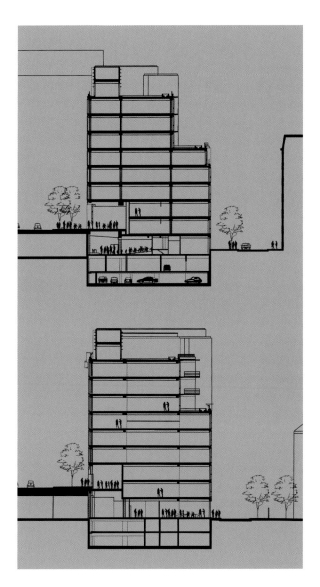

winner Christian de Portzamparc, a new boulevard, the Avenue de France, has been created on a concrete platform built over the railway tracks that lead to the Gare d'Austerlitz. It is at the edge of this platform that Valode & Pistre designed the future Transpac headquarters for the promoter Meunier. Located near Le Corbusier's *Cité-Refuge de l'Armée du Salut* (Salvation Army Refuge, 1933), the Transpac building may have more to do with the Flatiron Building in New York than with early French modernism, at least where its rounded prow is concerned. The architects dealt here with a relatively difficult site composed of two essentially triangular elements meeting at the tips, and an 8-meter gap between the level of the concrete platform and the neighboring streets. Stone façades on the rear of the building with gardens are a bow to neighboring older buildings on the rue Edmond Flamand, while the two sections of the building are connected by a set of transparent walkways and staircases. The cafeteria of the complex opens toward existing trees at the rear of the building, giving users the impression of being more integrated into the neigh-

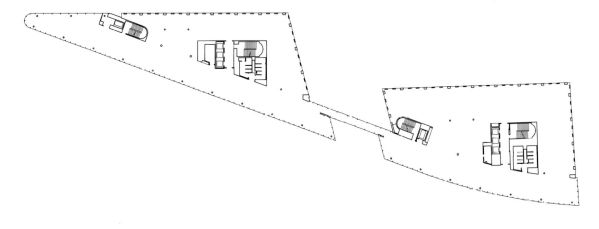

The central passageway, with its double Fontainebleau-style staircase offers a hint of transparency that the mass of the structure might otherwise not reveal. The glassed-in bridges between the two buildings also recall the earlier subway bridge seen in the image on this page, above, right.

borhood than they might otherwise be. Between the new boulevard, the substantial difference in street level on one side of the building and the other, and the proximity of an elevated subway line, it must be said that this was an extremely complex site in terms of dealing with the surroundings in a sensitive way, while designing an efficient and modern building. Valode & Pistre appear to have done exactly that, in fact their work might be considered an exemplary case of urban integration of a new structure. Although the Transpac building is no skyscraper the reference by the architects to the Flatiron Building has a specific logic. Set at the narrow diagonal angle formed by Fifth Avenue and Broadway, the rounded front of the New York structure is an early and successful attempt to integrate a modern building into its urban location. In the Seine Rive Gauche area, few architects have even attempted the type of contextual design seen in the Transpac building. This in itself is a tribute to the talents and the preoccupations of Valode & Pistre. ∎

# Havas Headquarters

| SURESNES - FRANCE |

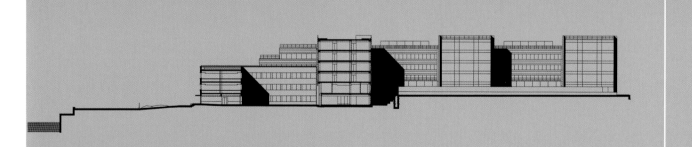

Completion date **2003**

Floor area **22,800 m²**

Client **Hines**

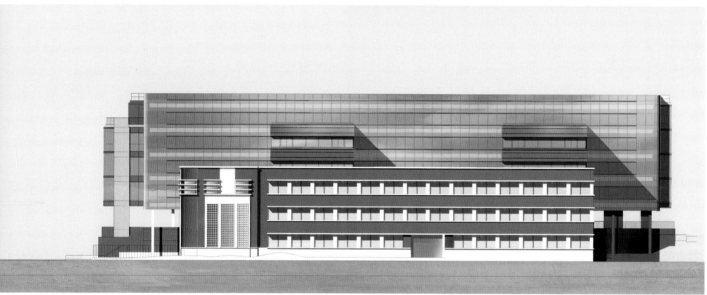

The former Coty factory is integrated into the new Havas complex with subtlety and intelligence. In the view from the Seine, it is obvious that the choice of materials for the new parts of the building obviates its larger volume, allowing the old factory to set the scale and rhythm of the design.

■ This interesting project for a site on the Seine River near Paris was undertaken by Valode & Pistre for the US real estate developer Hines. Hines is well known for the quality of their projects. Denis Valode emphasizes that Hines agreed to all of the architects' proposals, even when extra cost was involved. An existing building, the Coty perfume factory built by Jean Barrot in 1939, thus became an integral part of their design. The modern style brick, concrete and glass structure could have been demolished, but Valode & Pistre chose to retain it. "We had what I would call a 'Chateau de Versailles' instinct," says Jean Pistre, explaining that it was King Louis XIV. who insisted on keeping the original Louis XIII. hunting pavilion that is at the heart of the much larger new castle. The riverside façade of the Coty factory was thus restored and the architects added 35,000 m² of new buildings behind it on the deep site. Just as in the case of the royal

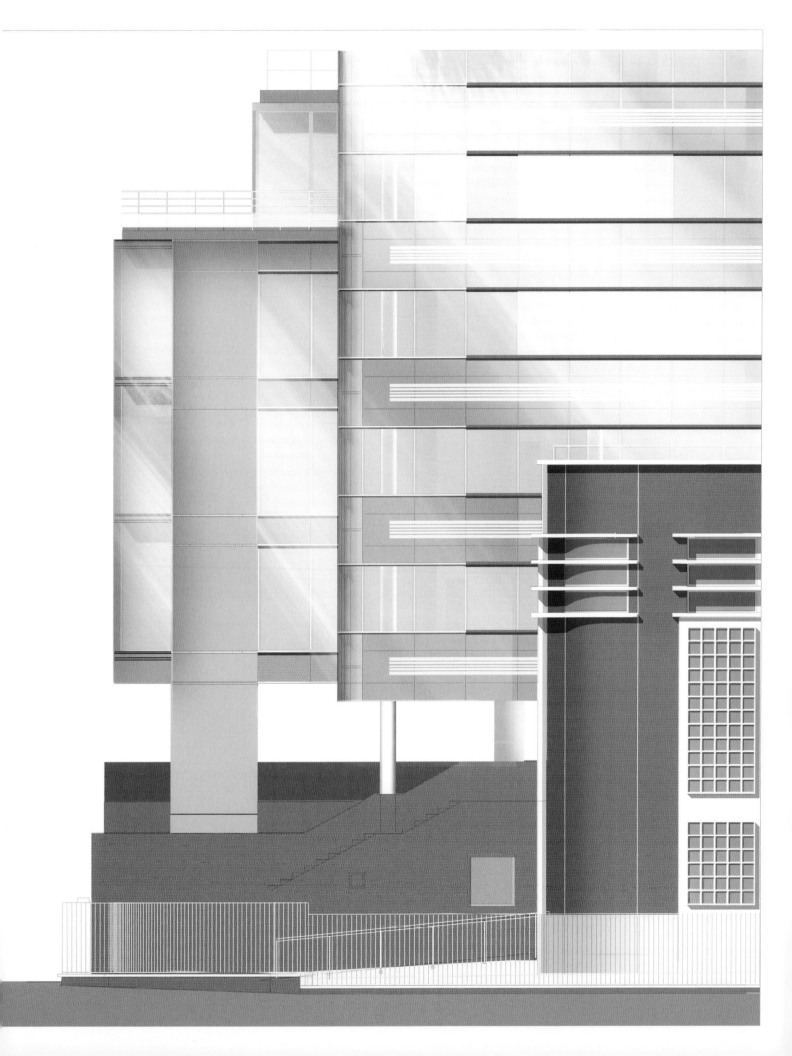

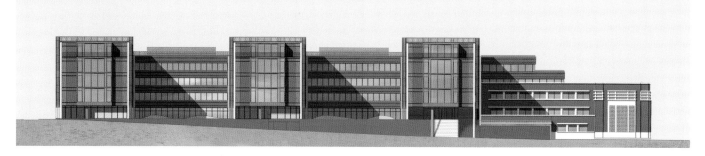

The larger blocks designed by Valode & Pistre are set on the street that is perpendicular to the Seine, concealing the fact that their floor area is vastly larger than the old factory. The division and articulation of the office blocks was designed with the possibility that there would be several clients before Havas came into the picture.

Entirely to their credit, the architects have carefully restored the Coty factory whose fundamental modernity is carried through in the contemporary shapes located further back from the river. The large windows on the Seine side give a spectacular setting to the conference room seen on this page, upper right.

castle at Versailles, a smaller, existing building became the core to which newer structures were added. The one disadvantage of the site was that a hotel of modest architectural quality had already been built in the rear corner of the lot. Although the buildings added by Valode & Pistre are quite large, the architects intentionally made them quite discreet on the street running perpendicularly to the Coty façade, using brick to emphasize the link with the older building and drawing the bulk of the structures back from the street. The original plan of Hines called for the possibility of renting space to several different companies, so the complex consists of several essentially independent blocks. Before the work had been completed however, the entire complex was rented to the large French advertising agency Havas. Working with company president Jacques Séguela, the architects engaged in a number of significant changes in the plans. A well known figure in France, Séguela is noted for his flamboyant presentation of advertising campaigns such as the one used by François Mitterrand when he became President of France ("La force tranquille"). "Séguela wanted us to create a kind of scenario where visiting clients could see

The architects have also worked on the interiors of the building, carrying through their elegant modernism in the choice of furniture and lighting. Spaces are ample and well lit, which surely contributes to the overall efficiency of the working environment.

As is often the case, Valode & Pistre give importance here to inner courtyards and gardens making the facility even more convivial than it might have been, had they insisted on a maximum degree of "useful" space. They succeed in giving nobility to working spaces that other architects sometimes ignore or treat in a less circumspect way.

the work of the company going on. The main gallery is at the heart of this concept, with a space intentionally designed for the signing of contracts once clients have been sufficiently impressed with the approach of Havas." Here, as in their campus designed for Cap Gemini / Ernst & Young, Valode & Pistre have succeeded in restoring an old building and transforming it into an integral part of the design of an extremely modern complex. Although Hines and Havas are certainly not in the perfume business, the decision to retain the Coty factory as part of the plan, underlines the history of the area, since Suresnes was the home of Fargeot, the perfumer of Marie-Antoinette. Almost more than this historical anecdote however, it is the very passion of Valode & Pistre for architecture, whether it be old or new that is apparent in the Havas project. They truly enjoyed renovating the Coty factory and making it an integral part of a coherent, contemporary whole. ∎

# Renault Technocentre, Le Gradient

| GUYANCOURT – FRANCE |

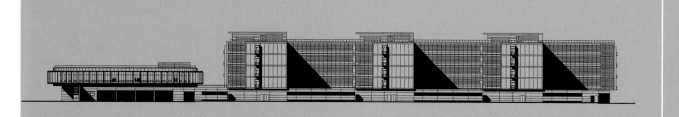

Completion date **2003**

Floor area **47,000 m²**

Client **Renault**

Selected by the president of the automobile manufacturer Renault after a limited consultation of four French firms (Sarfati, Architecture-Studio, Viguier and Valode & Pistre), Valode & Pistre laid out the master plan for the Renault Technocentre outside of Paris, described as a "city of research." Unlike other corporate research parks, the particularity of this one was that apart from Renault no other firm is involved, thus obviating the need to differentiate one company from its nearby rivals for example. The orthogonal layout of the complex allows for change or evolution while retaining the basic city-like organization. Denis Valode asks if the type of orthogonal system chosen by the firm for the urban plan is "Modern or Chinese, Spanish or Roman in its inspiration." The implication is that Valode & Pistre here call on very old ideas in order to make the most contemporary plan possible. Within the complex, Valode & Pistre were also chosen to build a computer sciences building called *Le Gradient*. Set against an artificial hill on the eastern edge of the site created when the Technocentre was first built, this building boasts one of the only circular forms of the complex, a round restaurant. Sloping upward to accompany

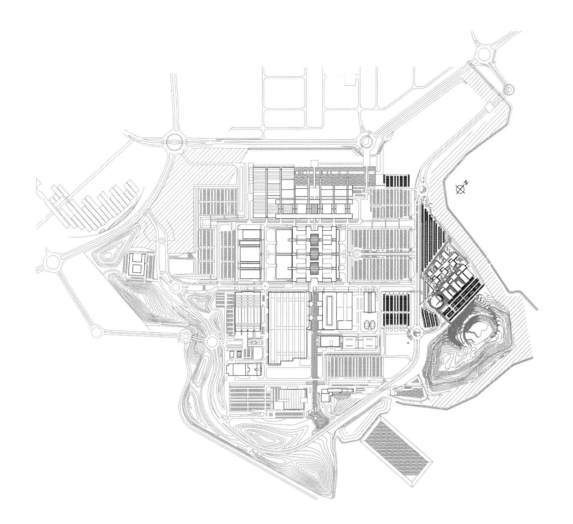

The cadenced massing of the complex has a rather military look about it in these images, but it is clear that Valode & Pistre are often selected by their clients because of the efficiency of their designs. An overall site plan shows the Gradient to the right, above.

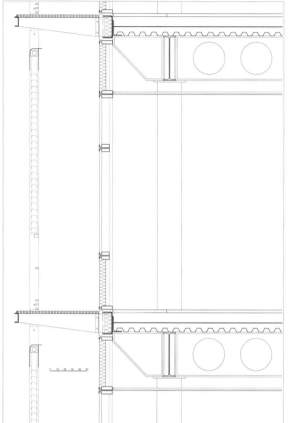

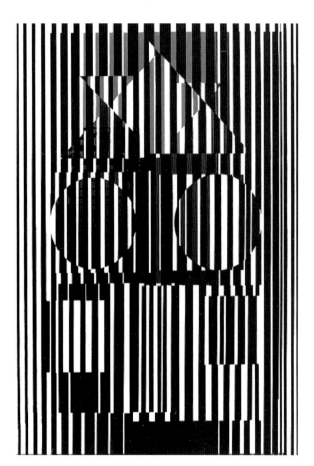

Sober but elegant,
the spaces of *Le Gradient*
rely on a sophisticated
use of materials and
engineering. As always,
ample glazing offers
views out of the building
to its users.

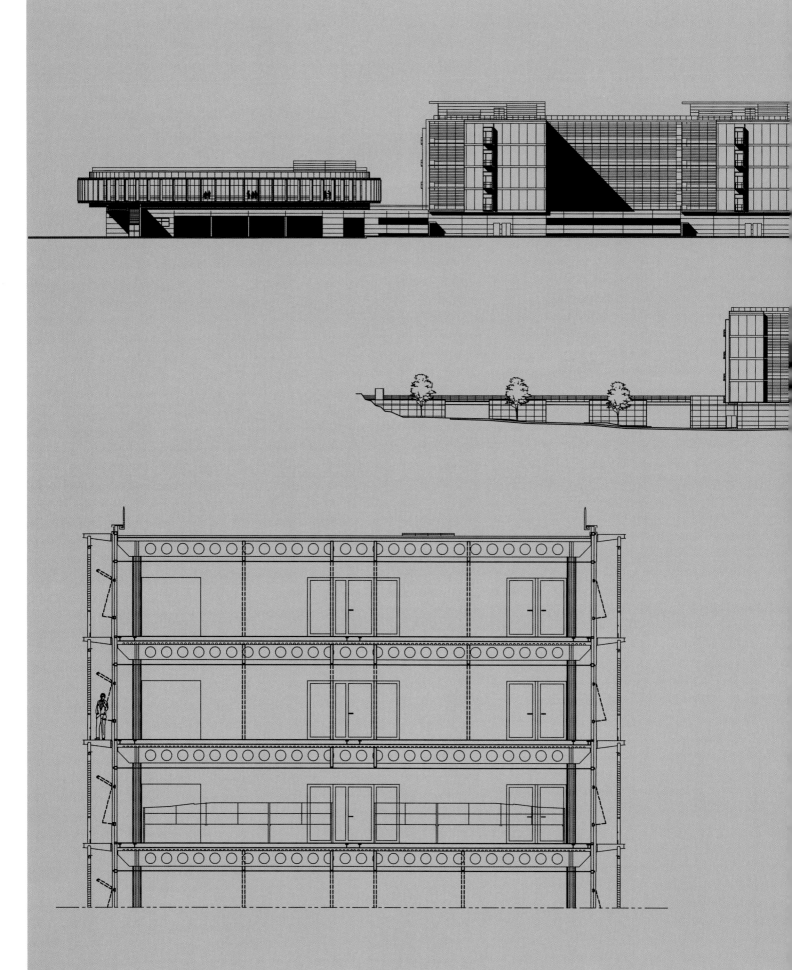

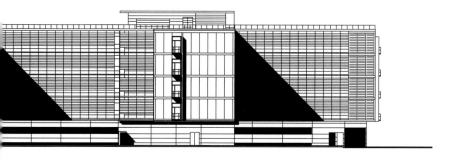

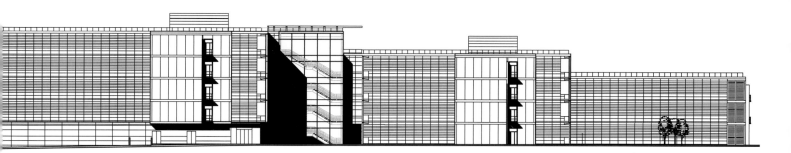

Essentially a repetitive scheme, the *Gradient* uses internal courtyards and a checkerboard plan to offer a maximum of exterior views from the offices. Light and efficient, the architecture is executed here in the service of an industrial goal – a situation that the architects do not reject.

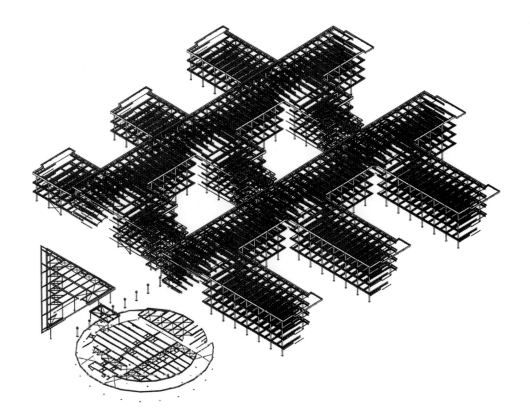

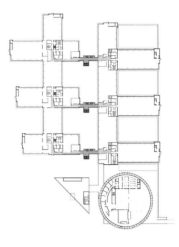

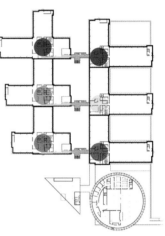

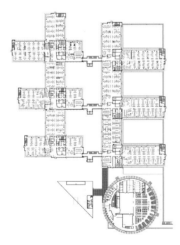

the hillside, the building has a clear topographic element, but remains essentially orthogonal and strictly logical in its organization. The structure opens onto a garden environment on the ground floor, and a long interior "street" cuts through from one end to the other, giving access to the vertical circulation cores and common spaces. As they have in other buildings the architects here insist on the value of a large free span that obviates the need for intermediate columns. An extensive use of aluminum cladding is characterized as a reference to the automobile industry, but otherwise, this building is a modern office complex that *owes* little of its inspiration to the client's activity.  Despite the great emphasis placed by Valode & Pistre on the quality of the working environment and its flexibility, they have used standardized construction materials throughout. The north-south alignment of the buildings has led the architects to carefully consider the matter of solar gain for the southern façade. They are also attentive to the competing desires to admit ample natural light to the building and yet to avoid computer screens becoming difficult to see.

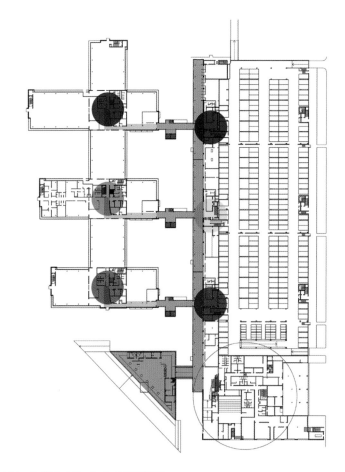

Massing and articulation of the complex allow users to orient themselves easily, despite the size of the complex.
An elegant combination of wood, steel and glass gives an almost luxurious aspect to the passageway seen below.

Ample ceiling heights
and floor to ceiling
glazing give an airiness
that is unusual in
modern office buildings.
There is an almost
Japanese sparseness
about the space seen on
the left.

Easy circulation throughout the buildings is insured by the overall design, and as Denis Valode explains, "We are obsessed by the idea that we are in a sense putting people on stage, and that we are responsible for their entrances and their exits." The architects have concentrated on offering what they call "binary choices" to users of the building – a simple matter of orientation, with views to the exterior that assure that no one will be lost in a "soulless" or sterile office environment. This attention to basic needs, together with the adaptation of *Le Gradient* to its natural setting, characterizes Valode & Pistre and sets them apart in the profession. Indeed many reputable architects neglect such obvious questions as how a given person will react to their working environment. Here, it is possible to concentrate on work precisely because time is not lost by looking for orientation or in dealing with unpleasant spaces. ■

# Las Mercedes Business Park

| MADRID – SPAIN |

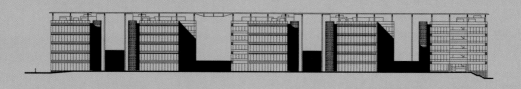

Completion date **2005**

Floor area **78,500 m²**

Client **Nexity España / Standard Life**

Associated architect **Reid Fenwick**

A repetitive massing with very high, light columns supporting a sunscreen roof allows size to become less apparent from the outside. The ample glazing reinforces an impression of lightness that is obviously a goal of the architects.

■ This ambitious speculative project forms an entire block located near the Barajas Airport of Madrid on a former industrial site, about 15 minutes by car away from the center. Bordered by four streets, one of them a busy artery leading into the heart of Madrid, the complex is rather turned inward than toward its relatively unattractive environment. Nine office buildings surround a central landscaped park, essentially forming a perimeter wall facing the streets and giving a sense of privacy or campus life to the users. Some of the T-shaped building volumes penetrate the central space, increasing the façade area facing onto the green center of the project. As it often happens, this project was developed by the architects with partners they had already worked with in the past, in this case, the Scottish investment firm Standard Life. Common facilities including a meeting room and service spaces serving the entire complex, while parking space and a connecting technical gallery link the buildings below ground and avoid the unsightly problem of vehicles parked in the central area. An umbrella-like system is used on the roofs to shield the buildings from Madrid's intense summer heat. Brise-soleil panels and verandas further

Seen in plan and section, there is an almost factory-like bulk to the complex, but the choice of materials, including the cladding and the insistent aerial grid obviate the appearance of aggressive efficiency that might have emerged were this project to have been in the hands of lesser architects.

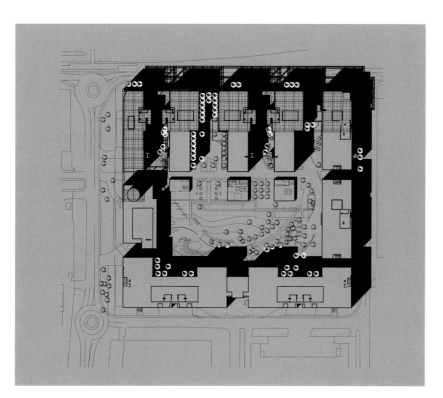

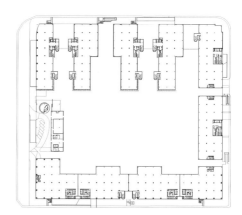

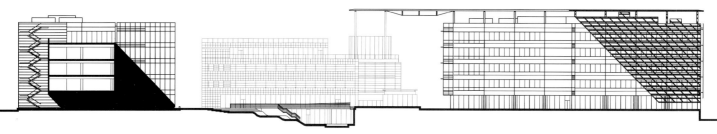

As they did in the Gradient, the architects break their pattern of rectilinear blocks with a round shape, that becomes a focal point on the edge of the group of buildings. An internal garden is seen from the maximum possible number of office windows.

accentuate the architectural response to climatic conditions. Despite the idea of a perimeter wall that shields the Business Park from the outside world, the high-columned umbrella design together with a more warmly colored round structure serving as a common facility for the entire complex do create an opening and an inviting prospect into the interior of the project. Working with a Spanish landscape architect, Valode & Pistre have intentionally given a Madrid flavor to the inner garden of the Las Mercedes Business Park, although their site is nowhere near some of its older historic models. Denis Valode emphasizes what he sees as some of the strong points in the project when he says, "This is basically a high-technology complex that offers nearly ideal working conditions to the companies that chose to work here. We have paid a great deal of attention to

Brise-soleils and the overhead grid shield the buildings somewhat from the strong Madrid sun. The transparency of the buildings co-exists with this willful protection offering the kind of contrast that the architects are particularly fond of.

the detailing of the buildings, and we have also tried to keep the whole complex sober and refined, using aluminum cladding and various spatial devices that make the whole inviting even though it is essentially turned in on itself." With their own office based in Madrid, Valode & Pistre have taken the time and the effort to design a complex that certainly meets international standards for office space at the same time as it responds to its rather difficult context and makes references, through the garden in particular to local traditions and spaces. As can be seen in almost all of their other projects, the architects put utmost emphasis on efficiency, modernity and contextual response, even when these factors take precedence over any expression of an overall style. The absence of a signature style, at least in outward appearances does not seem to have harmed their careers in any way, quite the contrary. ■

# T1 Office Tower

| LA DÉFENSE, PARIS – FRANCE |

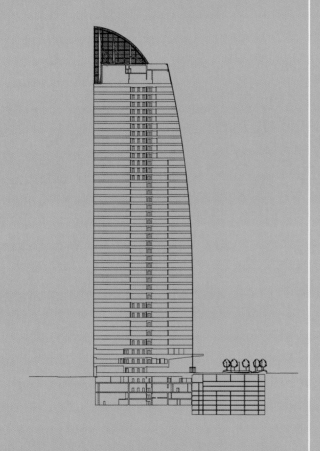

Completion date **2007**

Floor area **70,000 m²**

Client **Colony Capital-SITQ / Hines / Sesame**

Set at the edge of the Défense area, the T1 Tower breaks with the style of surrounding buildings, opting for an asymmetrical shape that gives a dynamic image even when seen from a considerable distance. Unlike many Défense buildings, caught in the elevated platform that excludes normal city life, T1 has one façade that is very much engaged with the urban movement of Courbevoie.

■ A number of talented architects have worked in the La Défense area of Paris, and the new T1 Tower designed by Valode & Pistre is to be located near the 183-meter high Granite Tower designed for the Société Générale by Pritzker Prize winner Christian de Portzamparc. Harry Cobb of Pei Cobb Freed is the author of other nearby buildings. The description given by Valode & Pistre of their building reveals a good deal about their design priorities: "T1 was conceived as a folded glass plate, 200 meters high, cut by an arc on its north face. The distinctive profile changes according to one's vantage point and assures the tower's insertion within the surrounding context. Seen from the south, the tower appears as a ship's bow, a vertical element and a complement to the skyline of the La Défense business district. Seen from the east and west, T1 is perceived as a large sail, its curving form providing transition to the lower scale of the adjoining neighborhood." Set to be the tallest building in the vicinity, T1 is located at the edge of the platform that most of La Défense is built on. It is there-

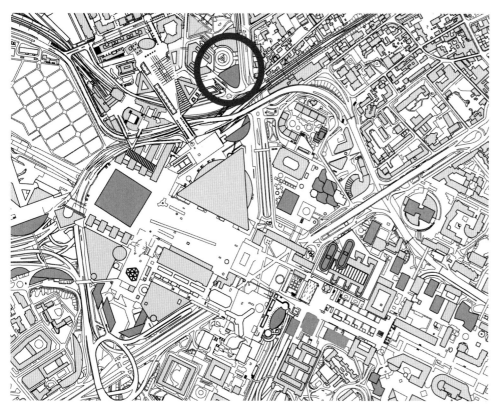

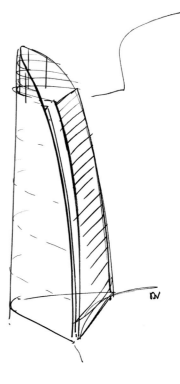

The architects are fond of citing examples to explain the evolution of the forms of their buildings. In the case of T1, an America's Cup class sailing boat, New York's Flatiron Building, or a snow-covered mountain, are the chosen references. Like a shining lighthouse, the building will stand out from its environment.

These references are
more than superficial,
since they situate the
design both in the
context of design and
architecture as well as
that of natural forms.

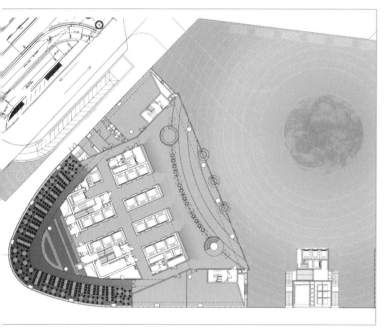 

The T1 project involves
a second, smaller
structure, whose curved
façade echoes that
of the tower and
simultaneously forms
a small urban park.

fore at the juncture between a modern purpose-built business environment and the older town of Courbevoie. Referring to the Flatiron Building
in New York, America's Cup sailing vessels and the naturally chiseled form
of an iceberg, the architects seek, as they usually do, to identify their proposals by comparison with known shapes, either from architectural or
natural vocabularies. Perhaps because they were working here with the
US firm, Colony Capital, Denis Valode compares the summit of T1 to
another iconic American image: "It's intended to hide the technical facilities located on the roof," says the architect. "The shape we designed looks
like the head of the Statue of Liberty with the rays coming out of its crown.
The tower becomes a figure, and the figure is wearing a crown. This idea
fits in with our system of references, but it is also related to the concept
itself." The essential elements of the design do influence appearance, but
they are also based on an understanding of engineering and the practical aspects of creating office space. In this tower, the floors have a more
or less constant net floor area, the curve of the structure and diminish-
ing profile being due to the fact that fewer technical installations such as

Floor to ceiling glazing
and the basic, sweeping
curve of the plan offer
spectacular views
toward La Défense
and Paris itself. Core
services are elegantly
concentrated in the
ovoid plan, giving
a maximum amount
of usable space
to each floor.

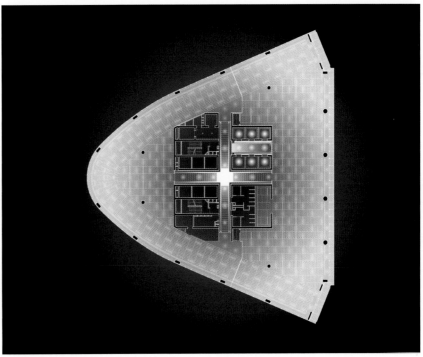

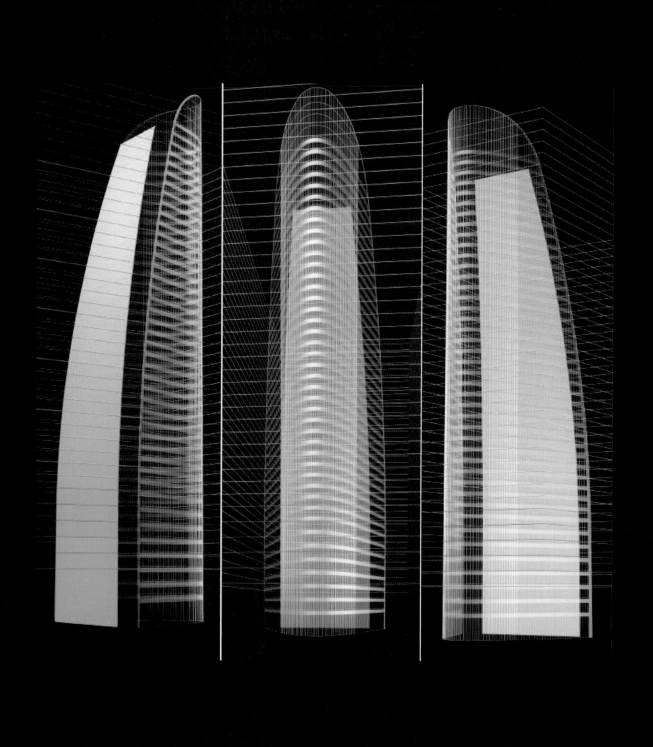

elevator cores are required in the upper reaches of a 200-meter high building. T1 and a smaller office block also designed by Valode & Pistre for the site are separated by a small square that Denis Valode compares to a "Place Furstemburg in the round," likening its shape to the famous square in the Saint-Germain-des-Prés area of Paris. In the design of this square, partially dictated by the urban plan of Roland Castro, as in the T1 Tower itself, Valode & Pistre show a particular interest in an economy of means and an efficiency that honors them. "We are convinced that the role of the architect is to do more with less and not the contrary," says Denis Valode. "Finding the exact means required to achieve a given purpose is essential. Using enormous means to create a small event is neither in the logic of construction nor of architecture. Our goal is to give the best final result with a certain economy of means." ∎

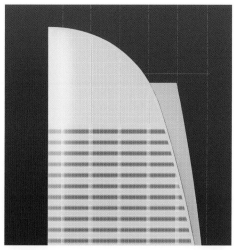

Significantly, the shapes of the T1 Tower are extremely simple. The architects do not seek to innovate for the sake of innovation and certainly not in the hope of creating a superficial "thrill" – rather they succeed in reconciling excellent design with industrial efficiency.

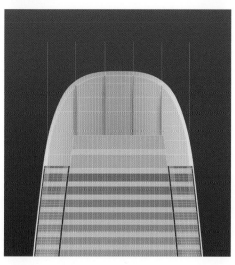

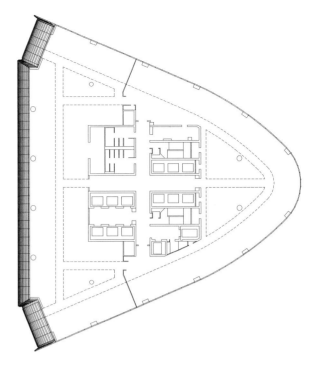

Carefully designed to be able to withstand potentially considerable winds, the sail-like top of the building is one of its signature features, forming its visible profile and giving an impression of even greater height than that of the actual structure. Light and translucent, this contemporary version of the cresting seen on Second Empire French architecture gives much of its particular character to the T1 Tower.

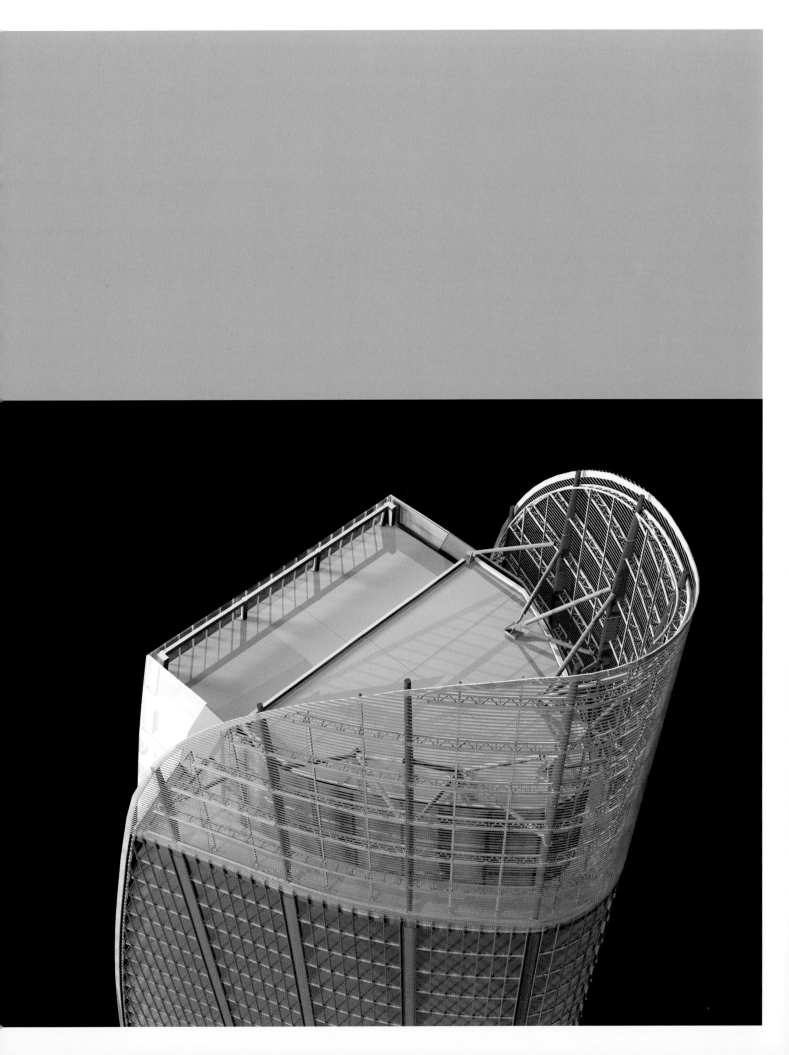

# Beaugrenelle Shopping Center

| PARIS - FRANCE |

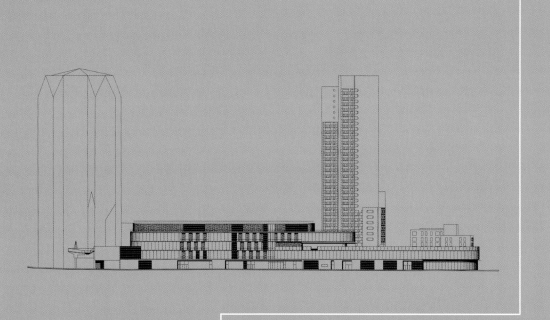

Completion date **2007**

Floor area **75,000 m²**

Program **Shopping center, mutiplex movie theater, restaurants**

Client **SCI Beaugrenelle APSYS-GECINA**

Winners of a 2002 competition organized by local authorities for architects associated with promoters, Valode & Pistre have again undertaken the renovation, or rather the reconstruction of modern buildings that no longer serve their initial purpose well. The Beaugrenelle shopping center, located in the Front de Seine area of the 15th arrondissement in Paris is a leftover from the late 1960's era of Georges Pompidou's attempt to modernize the city. As surprising as it may be to anybody but the French, Beaugrenelle was also the object of an intervention by the President who succeeded Pompidou, Valéry Giscard d'Estaing, who wished for the complex to be less brutally modern and more "picturesque" as Denis Valode puts it. The result of so much government meddling was a shopping center that no longer attracted many clients. One of the first ideas of the architects was to slice through a huge concrete platform that had covered a street, turning one of the prime access routes to the area into a dark tunnel. A light bridge will link the two main blocks of the complex, replacing the thick concrete platform. Continuous, aligned façades will replace the heterogeneous mixture that had come to characterize the complex. Valode & Pistre have also restored a more normal mixture of pedestrian and vehicular traffic whereas the earlier concept had attempted to entirely

Located along the river, but inserted into the decidedly un-Parisian Front de Seine area of modern towers, the Beaugrenelle complex offers a very central location and the considerable challenge of updating largely failed 1960's architecture.

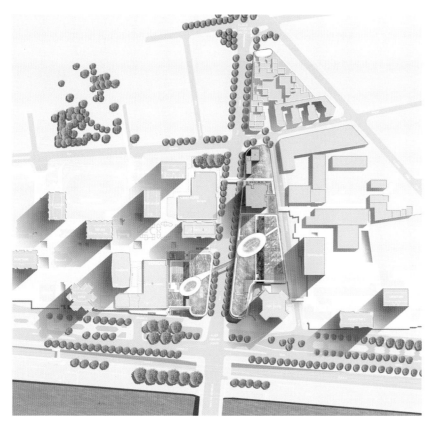

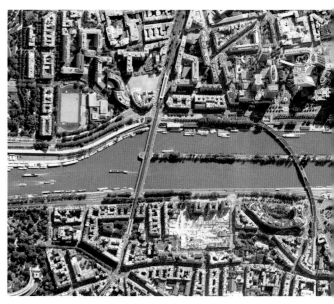

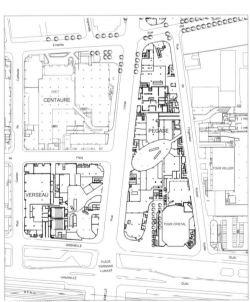

From a symbol of
concrete heaviness, the
architects seek to
extract a new lightness
born of ample glazing
and lighting destined to
attract shoppers back
to an area that they had
long-since abandoned.

Garden spaces and greenery help the architects to redevelop the Beaugrenelle complex in the midst of a largely depressing set of skyscrapers. Their insistence on this natural image is seen in their selection of reference images, above.

separate the two, creating uninviting ground level spaces that are usually prime locations for boutiques and shops. Within the center, an atrium and a strongly marked diagonal axis make it easier for pedestrians to look into the complex and to understand where they can go. After originally proposing large-scale "super graphic" inscription of the words "Beaugrenelle" on the glass façades, the architects decided to call on the Swiss artist Rémy Zaugg who has worked frequently with Herzog & de Meuron to create a work which will identify and characterize the complex through a varied presence of images and words on the exterior glazing. These will be mixed with a limited number of signs for the stores located in Beaugrenelle. As the artist says, "The work will give a human and poetic identity to the site, by addressing itself at one moment to private individuals in a sensitive, and why not sentimental way, and at other moments to the city itself." Although these words don't give a clear idea of the final appearance of the building, the overall idea of the architects is to convert an essentially brutalist and dysfunctional shopping center into a pleasant space that once again makes the city agreeable and easy to understand. Analogous to their PB12 project in the sense that it seeks to undo the modernist excesses of Paris in the late 1960's and early 1970's, the Beaugrenelle complex will be another example of just how sensitive and truly modern Valode & Pistre are. They certainly place more importance on the functional success and attractiveness of their projects than they do on any ego-driven signature architecture. ∎

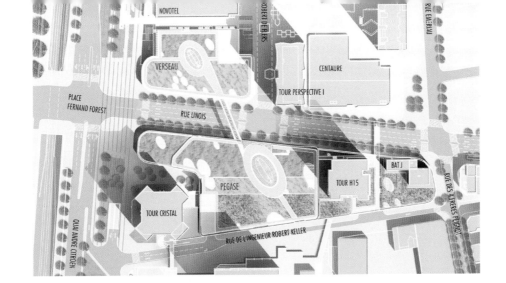

# Hyatt Hotel

| EKATERINBURG - RUSSIA |

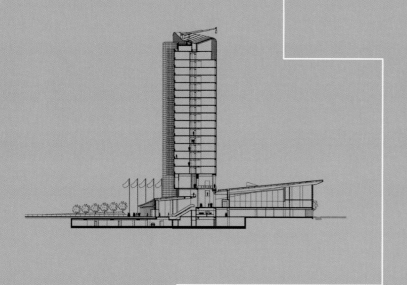

Completion date **2008**

Floor area **31,000 m²**

Program **250-room hotel, fitness center and convention facilities**

Client **Ural Mining and Metallurgical Company**
**Bouygues Bâtiment International**

The architects have been called on to design a scheme that may well lead them to participating in a larger manner in the urban development of the city (right). As it stands, alone, the hotel tower looks like a delicately carved slice of ice, a kind of focal point for a city that gets very cold indeed in winter.

The city of Ekaterinburg was founded in 1723 at the limits between Asia and the Urals as a stronghold for Peter the Great's colonization of the region and Siberia. As the industrial and military center of the Mining Administration, it immediately took on a great importance that continued throughout the Soviet era, when the city was renamed Sverdlovsk. Entirely closed to outsiders between 1960 and 1990, it nonetheless maintained high academic standards, with more than 100 research institutes and 15 establishments of higher education. It has a rich tradition of industrial architecture as well as a number of structures related to the Constructivist movement. With a population of 1.5 million, the third largest city in Russia, again called Ekaterinburg has begun to open itself and it was the city that solicited Valode & Pistre together with the construction company Bouygues to design a world-class hotel. It should be underlined that the French architects regularly hold an internal design competition open to their own architects. The stunning design for the Hyatt Hotel in Ekaterinburg is the work of the winner of the 2004 competition, Valérie Vaconsin. By the standards of many large architectural offices, Valode & Pistre have a relaxed and quite young group of collaborators. The fact that a young internal competition winner was selected to design such an

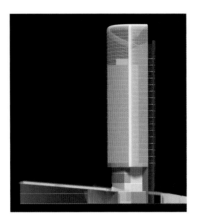

A testimony to the quality of architects working on the staff of Valode & Pistre, the hotel is a layered composition sitting in one corner of an essentially square lot. All of the rooms face the cathedral and the mountains in the distance.

important project, and that her name is cited in reference to the hotel, is an exceptional proof of openness. All 250 rooms in the 18-story tower, 80-meter high hotel are located on the side of the Iset River and offer a panoramic view of the distant mountain forests. The curved glass façade that gives the building an appearance likened by the architects to an "ice cube," poses a certain number of technical problems related to condensation, given the temperature extremes of Ekaterinburg. These are solved using double or triple paned glass with inert gas between the layers. The idea of an ice cube is in fact a nod to a strong local tradition – that of an annual ice sculpture competition. The view to the river also highlights another local high point; the cathedral dedicated to the last Czar Nicholas II. and his family. The axial arrangement of the hotel itself and the surrounding area for office buildings that is also to be developed by Valode & Pistre is directly related to the presence of the cathedral. The inner façade of the building, facing away from the river is more closed and is clad in stone, copper and glass. In terms of its facilities, the Hyatt Hotel offers a number of surprises including a 25-meter indoor swimming pool on the top floor and a monumental entrance hall. Restaurants located 15 meters above the entry level open out to roof gardens during summer. A large convention facility is also located in the base of the tower. The contrast between the glazed perfection of the exterior of the structure and the warmth of the interior of the hotel suggests the idea of "fire beneath the ice" according to Denis Valode. ∎

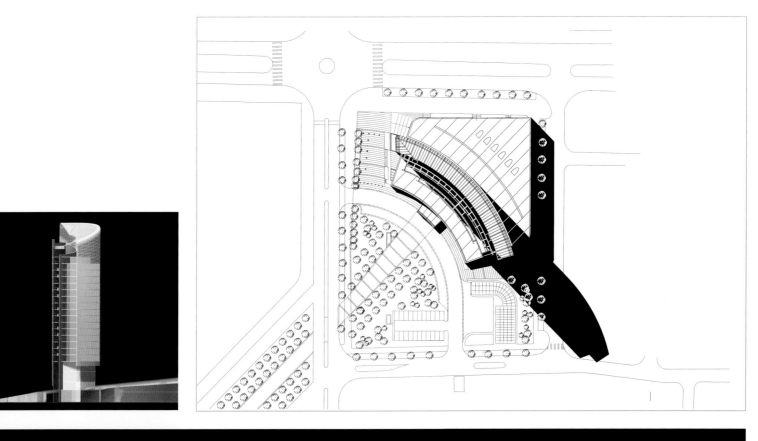

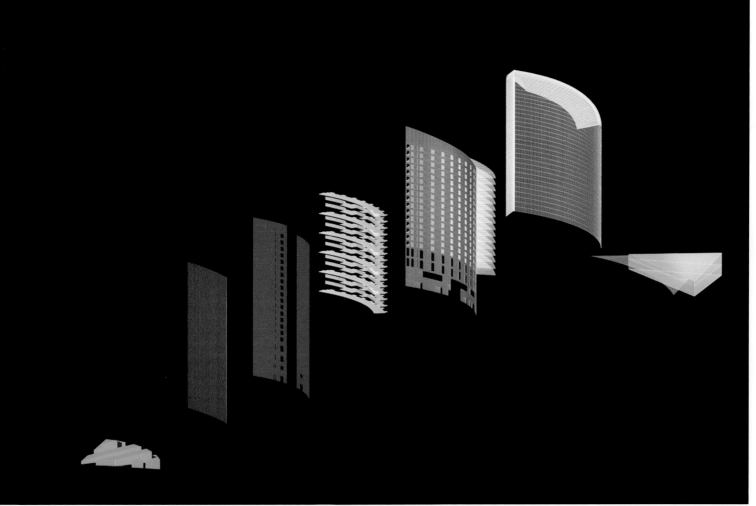

Concentrated on the frontal curved façade, the guest rooms are set atop a triangular base. It is interesting that although this project was not the result of direct work by the firm's principals, it does quite successfully embody their own ideas of modern simplicity and elegance.

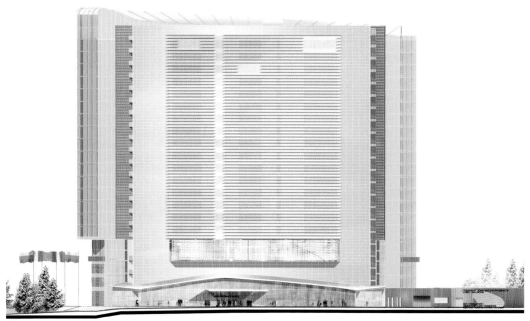

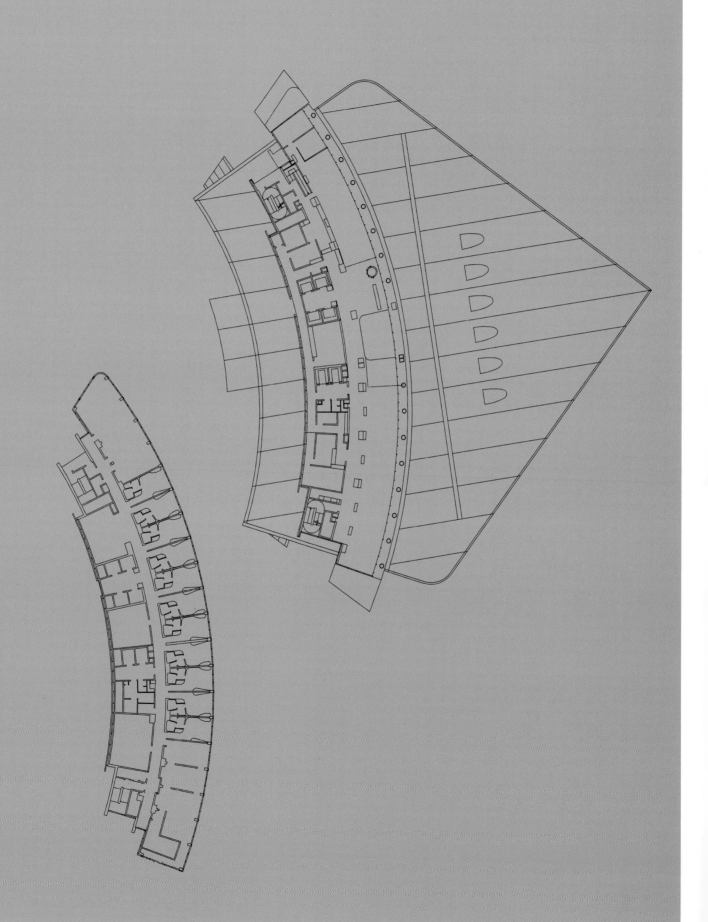

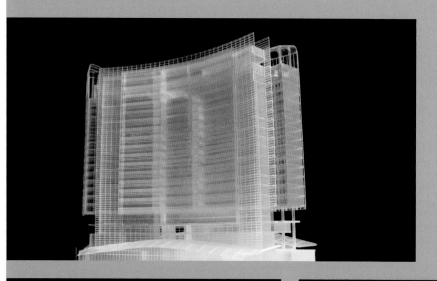

Paying careful attention to local sensitivities, the architects have aligned the hotel toward the cathedral dedicated to the last Czar of Russia. Light and airy, the curved structure faces complex technical problems posed by a glass structure that has to undergo extremes of temperature both in summer and in winter.

# Jiuxianqiao

| BEIJING - CHINA |

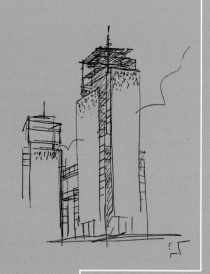

Completion date **2008**

Complete floor area  **156,500 m²**
Offices  **87,000 m²**
Apartments  **40,000 m²**
Commercial  **22,500 m²**
Hotel  **7,000 m²**

Client  **Beijing Capital Land**

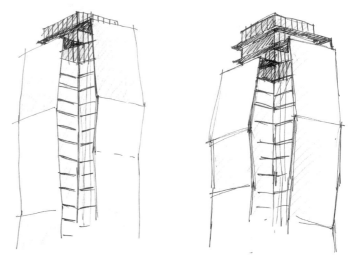

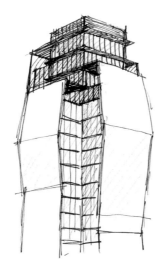

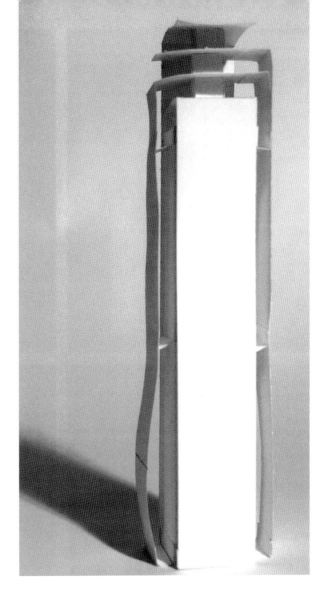

Like an unfurled parchment, with an abstract pattern based on Chinese ideograms, the cladding of the towers is their signature feature, distinguishing them from almost any other new Beijing architecture. Again, the architects stick to rectilinear basics when it comes to floor plans, but they offer a seductive solution to the problem posed by China's desire for a "local" flavor.

■ The innovative methods used by Valode & Pistre with some success have also permitted them to obtain commissions far from France. One of the bigger of these is a complex of five buildings located in north-eastern Beijing. Called Jiuxianqiao, the group of towers measuring respectively 150 and 100 meters in height will house offices, apartments, commercial space and a hotel. The two office towers will be the first elements built, and since they are the tallest of the group, they will become the symbols of Jiuxianqiao. Denis Valode explains, "We were not looking for what you might call a 'Chinese style,' but rather for a contemporary interpretation of Chinese culture. We turned to writing and more precisely ideograms and the carved stone blocks that were used to print in the distant past. Of course we have not used actual characters, but rather an undulating stone cut out façade that takes its inspiration from that source." The openings in these façades, which stand apart from the actual glazed building surfaces, are designed to deal efficiently with solar gain. The towers culminate in belvederes that offer a spectacular view on the capital city. The two housing towers and a mixed-use structure will be built at a later date, but the entire composition may be related to some extent to Beijing's Five Pagoda Temple. Originally known as the Temple of the True Awakening

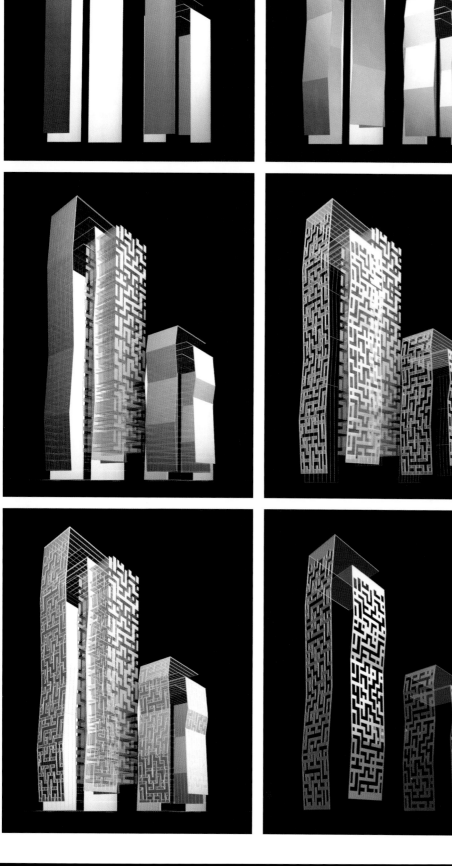

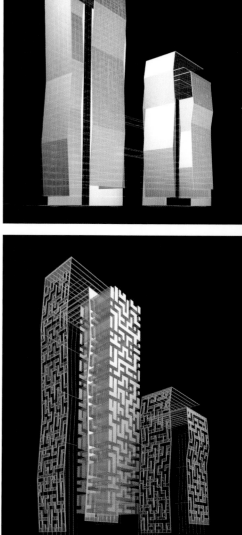

In the aerial view of the Chinese capital above, the Forbidden City is the dark area left of center, while the Valode & Pistre site is marked by a white circle. To the left, drawings emphasize the abstract character of the towers' cladding, almost like a stylized version of the city's own geometric variations.

(Zhenjuesi), this complex is located near the Beijing Zoo and was built in 1473 (only one extant structure dates from that period however). In an interesting twist of history, it happens that the original temples were almost entirely looted and burned to the ground by the Anglo-French allied armies in 1860. Valode & Pistre have systematically used such references, not as direct sources for their designs, but rather to give clients and others called upon to judge their work a point of comparison that can be easily understood. Images of the specific sources of their ideas are included in their presentation brochures and exhibitions of their work. In no danger of designing in a Post-Modern pastiche style, their work is more thoughtful and abstract than derivative. Knowing full well that the Chinese have been struggling to find a "Chinese way" if not a specific style for their

A site plan, to the right, reveals the strict geometric massing of the buildings, belied only by their cleverly patterned skins. Also visible in the plan, the architects' response to the difficult conjunction on the site of the north-south and diagonal axes of Beijing.

burgeoning urban construction, the French architects have cleverly taken obvious cultural elements and reworked them in an abstract way, giving both modernity and a hint of rapport with the past which is truly appealing to the clients. Although their civilization is not as old as that of China, the French clearly must adapt their own modern construction to certain historic references. This fact permits them to have a more natural dialogue with their clients than Americans for example, although the Chinese are currently calling on architects from all over the world. Aside from such essentially esthetic concerns, the architects also pay careful attention to the site and its implications. The layout of the Jiuxianqiao buildings for example responds to the fact that on this particular site a diagonal grid meets the basic north-south alignment of most of the city. ∎

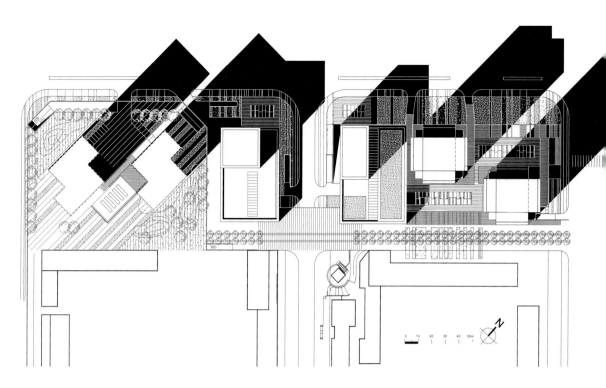

# Glasgow Graving Docks

| GLASGOW - SCOTLAND |

Completion date **2008**

Complete floor area **75,000 m²**
Hotel **15,500 m²**
Retail / leisure **6,700 m²**
Residential **41,300 m²**
Offices **11,500 m²**

Client **City Canal Limited**

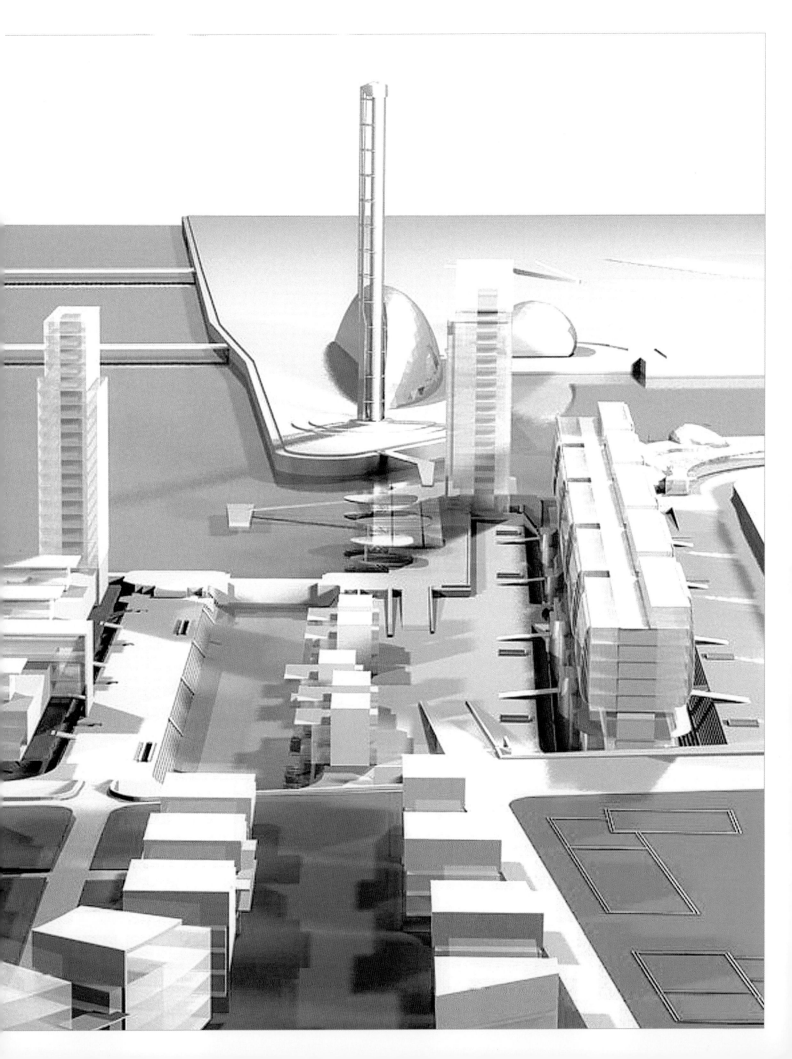

Again, handling
a historic context with
remarkable agility,
considering that
Scottish traditions
are not usually very
familiar to French
architects, Valode
& Pistre have suggested
a partial reuse of the
Graving Docks, and
new architecture that
blends easily with
the unusual site.

Glasgow of course has a strong architectural tradition thanks to figures such as Charles Rennie Mackintosh (1868-1928). In recent years, along the banks of the Clyde an effort has been made to turn largely abandoned industrial areas into attractive tourist and business centers. Norman Foster's Scottish Exhibition and Conference Centre (SECC), the Clyde Auditorium was completed in 1997 and more recently the Building Design Partnership (BDP) completed a Science Center and IMAX Cinema together with the 100-meter Glasgow Tower (original design by Richard Horden). In the 19th century, Glasgow became an international port and shipbuilding on the Clyde demanded numerous facilities. Tod & MacGregor built the first "graving dock" or dry dock for the Clyde Navigation Trust at Meadowside in 1858. Between 1875 and 1898 three more graving docks were built at a site called Govan, located just across the Clyde today from the SECC and even closer to the Science Center. The dock 3 was large enough to handle any ship in the world when it was finished, but shipbuilding on the Clyde did not really survive into the modern era, however, its 19th century architectural legacy remained. Associated with the local firm McGurn Architects, Valode & Pistre have conceived the master plan for the redevelopment of the Glasgow Graving Docks, taking into account the restoration of the dock 2 or middle dock with its impressive timber structure. Their plans call for the other two docks to be filled in and built

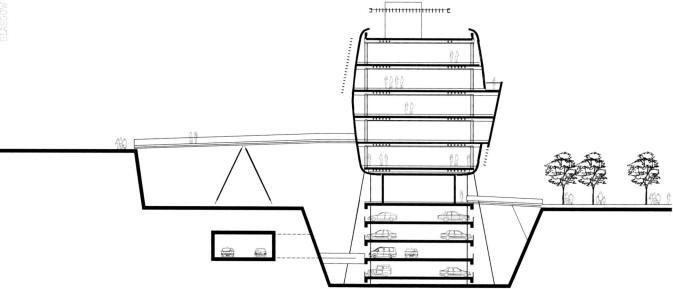

Above, a section shows
how a new building sits
like a ship in the
depression formed
by the former docks.
Part of an ambitious
series of projects
intended to reinvigorate
old Glasgow, the Graving
Docks scheme flows into
the abandoned waterside
site with an ease and an
appropriate fluidity.

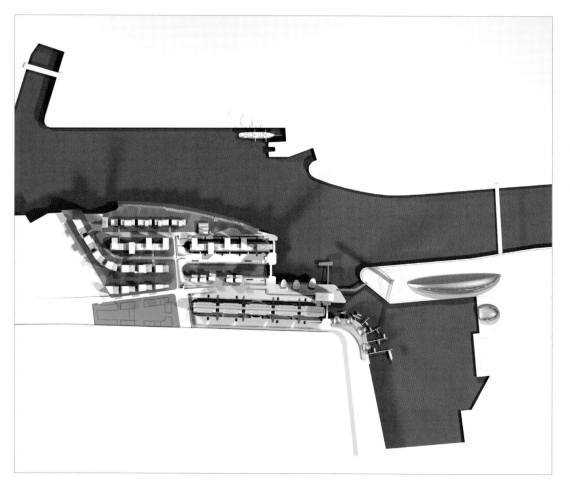

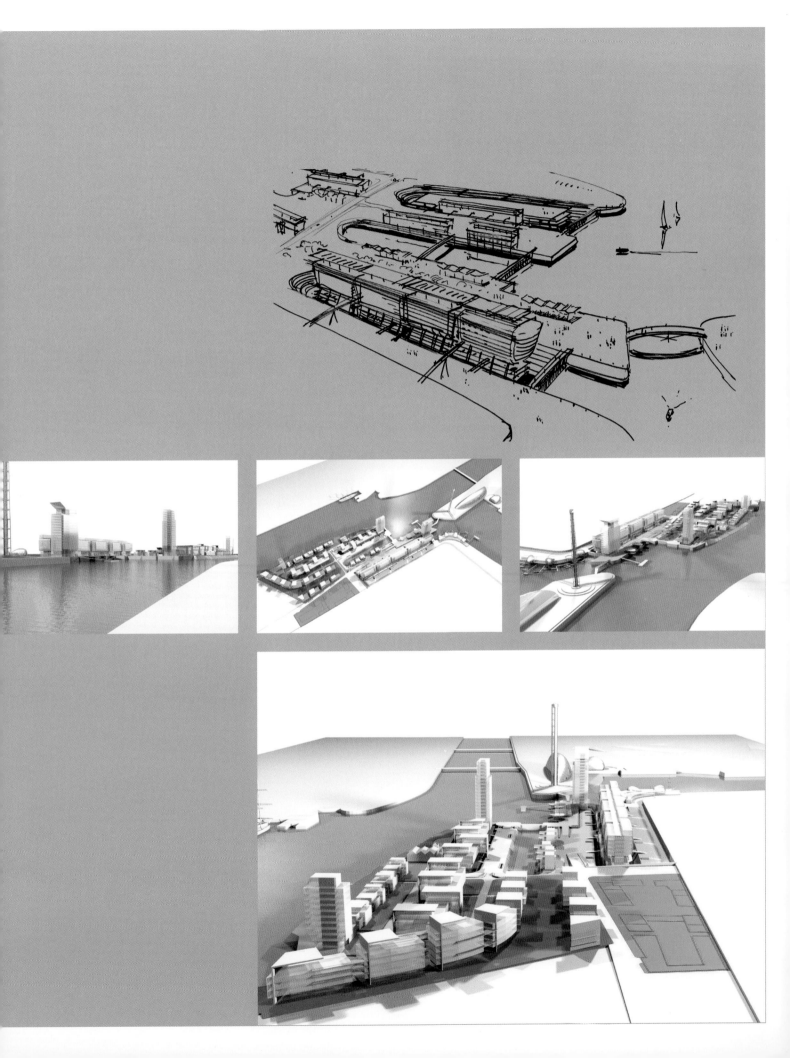

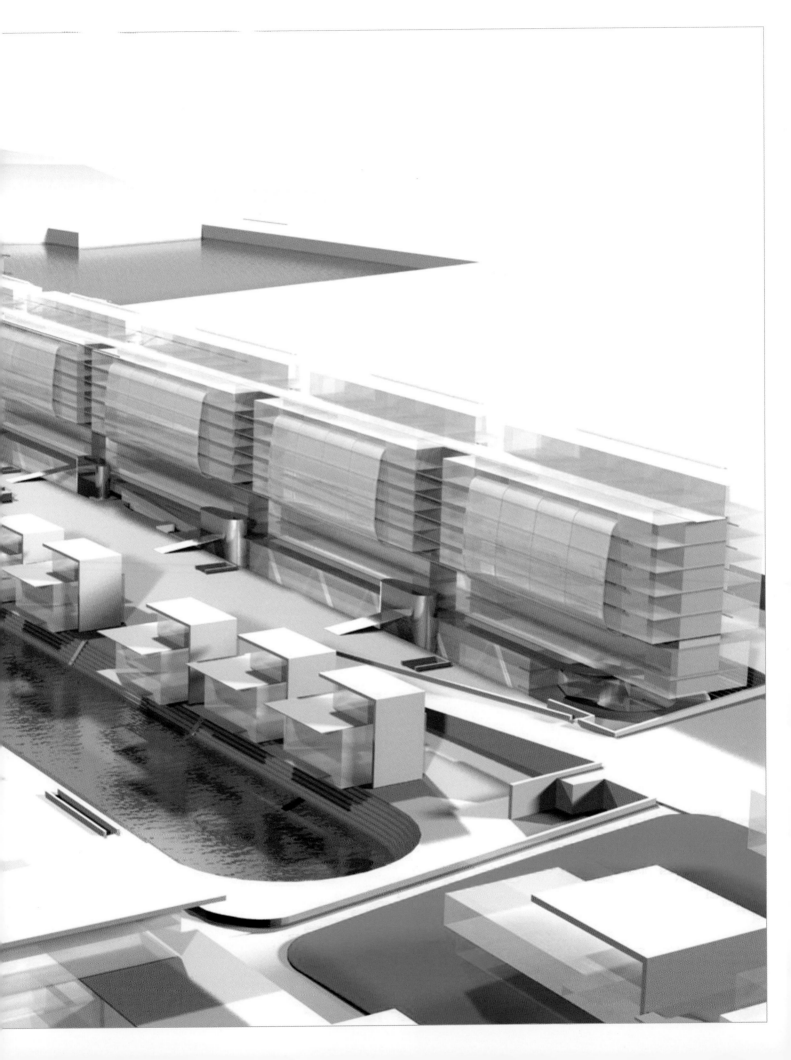

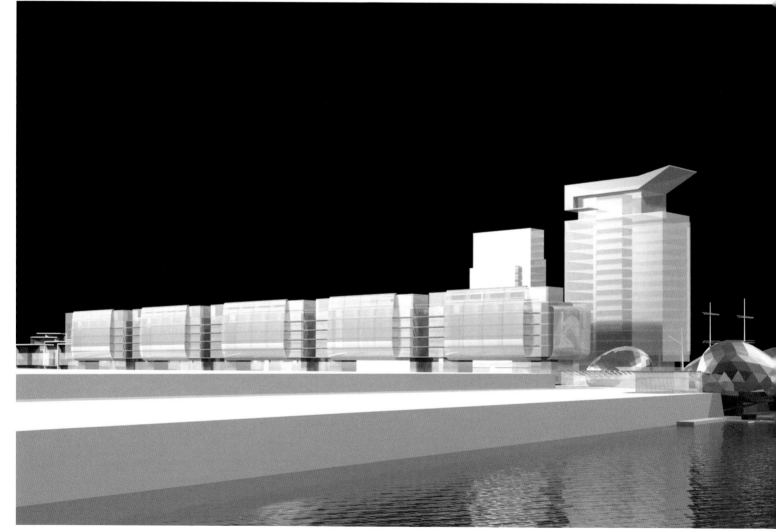

Sitting just opposite the somewhat controversial Glasgow Tower, a signature 14-story hotel stands out from the rest of the Valode & Pistre scheme. As is often the case in their projects, a rather strict set of identical blocks (below) leads up to this climax.

on. Empty for more than 20 years, the 81,600 m² site will include a hotel, retail / leisure, residential and office space. The leisure and retail zone is to be located near dock 2. Set across from the Glasgow Tower, a 14-story high rise will contain the 300-room hotel. On the whole, the buildings have a slightly ship-like appearance, their prows to the river, as might seem appropriate for this location. In all the five-year program calls for a total of 75,000 m² of new construction. Together with the other facilities already built or planned in the area such as a new headquarters for BBC Scotland, the Graving Docks project promises to be a center of life and activity on the riverside. Although located just 3 kilometers from Glasgow's Central Station, this area was more of a blight on the city than an asset just a few years ago. Despite their state of disrepair, the Secretary of State for Scotland listed the Glasgow Graving Docks as buildings of special architectural or historic interest of the highest category (A) on May 15, 1987. Plans made by the city over the past few years and in particular a comprehensive conservation plan written in August 2001 by the Keillor Laurie Martin Partnership and the Glasgow Preservation Trust formed the basis for the detailed program on which the architects worked to create their own master plan for the area. Although involved in work on a difficult and historically sensitive site in a foreign country, Valode & Pistre have shown the same type of adaptive capacity to work with existing conditions, and respect for older architecture in Scotland as they have in France. ∎

Illustration Credits

Hervé ABBADIE
Michel AZOUS
Nicolas BOREL
Christophe DEMONFAUCON
Michel DENANCE
Georges FESSY
Benoit FOUGEIROL
André MORIN
Fernando URQUIJO

All illustrations have been provided by Valode & Pistre Architects.